D0458438

TRAGEDY PLUS TIME

A TRAGI-COMIC MEMOIR

ADAM CAYTON-HOLLAND

TOUCHSTONE

New York   London   Toronto   Sydney   New Delhi

Touchstone
An Imprint of Simon & Schuster, Inc.
1230 Avenue of the Americas
New York, NY 10020

First Touchstone hardcover edition August 2018

TOUCHSTONE and colophon are registered trademarks of Simon & Schuster, Inc.

For information about special discounts for bulk purchases,
please contact Simon & Schuster Special Sales at 1-866-506-1949
or business@simonandschuster.com.

The Simon & Schuster Speakers Bureau can bring authors to your live event.
For more information or to book an event, contact the Simon & Schuster Speakers
Bureau at 866-248-3049 or visit our website at www.simonspeakers.com.

Interior design by Erich Hobbing

Manufactured in the United States of America

1   3   5   7   9   10   8   6   4   2

Library of Congress Cataloging-in-Publication Data

Names: Cayton-Holland, Adam author.
Title: Tragedy plus time : a tragi-comic memoir / by Adam Cayton-Holland.
Description: First Touchstone hardcover edition. | New York : Touchstone, 2018.
Identifiers: LCCN 2017049067| ISBN 9781501170164 (hardcover) |
ISBN 9781501170171 (trade paper)
Subjects: LCSH: Cayton-Holland, Adam. | Cayton-Holland, Adam--Family. |
Comedians--United States--Biography. | Suicide victims--Family
relationships--United States. | Brothers and sisters--United States--Biography.
Classification: LCC PN2287.C39 A3 2018 | DDC 792.7/6028092 [B] --dc23
LC record available at https://lccn.loc.gov/2017049067

ISBN 978-1-5011-7016-4
ISBN 978-1-5011-7018-8 (ebook)

To the Hollands and the Caytons
and the Cayton-Hollands
and the animals and all those people

PROLOGUE

I'm sitting in the glassed-in conference room of Amazon Studios, Sherman Oaks Galleria adjacent. Behind me, cars rip by on the 405 like an unflinching river. In front of me, dozens of sharply dressed millennials clack away at their keyboards, furiously expanding an insatiable empire. They pay me no mind, as I sit here in this aquarium with my bottle of sparkling water. They must see twenty of me a day.

The walls on either side of me are dry-erase boards, floorboards to ceiling. There's a basket of markers on the table. They don't expect me to draw something, do they? Am I supposed to diagram our show? I'm not up for that kind of effort. If they are expecting some sort of a performance here, these Amazonians will be sorely disappointed. I've got no razzmatazz in me, no showmanship.

I'm eight years into my stand-up comedy career, taking a huge development meeting; ostensibly this is the biggest moment of my young career, the one I've been waiting for. A childhood spent obsessing over everything comedy, those hours in the newspaper backroom cracking jokes, the long nights at the open mics, the endless road trips for a shit one-nighter in some heartbreaking town—it's all led to this.

My two cohorts in the Denver comedy troupe the Grawlix and I have written a TV script called *Those Who Can't*. It's been making the rounds in Hollywood. We've pitched it to Comedy Central, Adult Swim, FX. There's been interest but no bites. But it's got "heat," our people tell us, whatever that means. And word on the "heat" is Amazon is intrigued.

So here I sit, waving the flag for Team Grawlix, my partners-in-dick-jokes back home in Denver. Today it's all on me.

I see the development duo make their way through the bullpen in front of me, a medley of business casual. There's always two: one to do the work, the other to congratulate him. They enter. We shake hands. They offer me more water, coffee, whatever I need. We make small talk, the obligatory bullshitting in which creative people sit opposite noncreative people and laugh at the noncreative people's bad jokes because they know there might be some money on the other end of the whole whorish exchange. Backgrounds, schooling, snapshots of lives that once mattered but now wither in the shadow of almighty Hollywood. Then we get down to business.

"So what's up with *Those Who Can't?*"

"Nothing," I report. "A few networks are considering it but no one has committed. It's available."

"It's such a funny script," the Amazonian says.

"I know it is," I say. "It's the funniest script you'll read all year. You should buy it."

I'm not myself. I'm cocky, an arrogance born of total indifference. Normally I'd be polite, deferential even. They would comment on my manners after I'd left, that nice boy from one of those middle flyover states. But today I'm reckless.

None of this feels real. Just another incomprehensible turn in a recent flurry. Do I want to sell this thing? Of course. Do I care if I don't? Not in the least. So what does it matter if these people throw me out of their office? Who cares if I punch the guy in the face and take a shit on the conference room table? What's a development meeting mean in the grand scheme? What's the point of making a fucking TV show? Suddenly this all feels so goddamned empty.

But my existential indifference, that cliché cache of a disaffected teen, is doing something else for me today. Suddenly, I'm talking their talk. I'm a goddamn shark in this aquarium. I'm becoming fluent in Hollywood asshole. And if there's one thing an asshole can't resist, it's another asshole.

"We'd love to buy it," he tells me, a bit taken aback by my audacity, no doubt, but also suddenly fully erect for the first time all quarter. "But we're already developing another high school script."

"Fuck that other script," I blurt out, a little Ari Gold learning to fly. "Our script is better than that script."

"Well, between you and me, they haven't even finished their first draft," he confesses.

"They haven't even finished their first draft?! We've got a script ready to go!"

He looks at his partner seated next to him. His partner nods. Ego padded.

"Can you make a pilot in Denver for fifty thousand dollars" he asks.

"We can make five pilots in Denver for fifty thousand," I say.

We shake hands. I leave. My manager calls me twenty minutes later.

"I don't know what you said in there but they want to buy *Those Who Can't*!"

"Really?!"

"Really!"

My manager laughs. I laugh. He says he'll call me later with more details. He hangs up. I smile, proud of myself, happy for the adventure my friends and I are about to embark upon. I think about the countless shows we put on in those dive bars and DIY spaces and art galleries, the audiences growing with each new iteration. I think about all the hours we spent making sketch-videos for free on the weekends, how we started out so sloppy and amateurish, how we were always tweaking, never satisfied, always pushing forward. And now we get to make our own TV show.

Then I burst into tears. I cry all the way down Ventura,

then the entire length of Cahuenga, from the Valley to my budget Ramada hotel room in West Hollywood. Big, choking, snotty sobs, the kind that steal your breath away. That suffocate you.

What a picture I must be: some sad, bearded bastard weeping in his economy rental, KDAY blasting nineties West Coast hip-hop on the radio. There's probably thirty people doing the exact same thing within a two-mile radius of me.

But none of them just sold a script!

Then again, none of them found their little sister's dead body ten days ago either, the gun in her hand, the trickle of blood down her blue lips, her tiny bird-bone body lying there in her bed, never to move again. My best friend, my little sister Lydia, gone. Just like that.

I'm a thirty-two-year-old stand-up comic from Denver who just sold his first Hollywood script.

I've never been more devastated.

TRAGEDY PLUS TIME

THE CHILDREN
WHO FELT THE WORLD

Lydia almost drowned when she was three. Slipped through her kiddie inner tube and shot to the bottom of the pool. We were supposed to be watching her, but my older sister Anna and I got distracted. I was seven. Anna was nine. It was bound to happen. When I turned around Lydia was gone. All I saw was a pastel inner tube bobbing on the surface. Then I looked down and saw Lydia flailing on the bottom of the pool, her little body warped and distorted through the water. Before I could act my mother, a non-swimmer, was in the pool, thrashing toward her youngest. She had been reading poolside. My mom fished Lydia out and lay her stomach-down on the hot concrete. She pounded on her tiny back until Lydia began coughing up mouthfuls of water, then came sputtering back to us. She was fine; scared, but alive. She began crying and my mom rocked her until she was calm.

It was an innocent mistake, but I blamed myself. I had been the one closest to Lydia in the pool. I nearly let my little sister drown. I wouldn't have been able to go on living had that happened. None of us would have. Not in the same manner, anyway. We would be forever haunted by that day, by that death. We would have carried it with us like a festering wound, like a disease that eventually overtakes you.

And while I was so grateful that Lydia was okay, that we were allowed to carry on unscathed, deep down, I was surprised. Secretly I had suspected things would go the other way. If not that day, then another. When I saw Lydia at the bottom of that pool it felt like a premonition. *Here it is,* I thought. *Here is your tragedy.* It confirmed my suspicions. That the world was full of injustice and cruelty and darkness. You could stave it off for a while, but it was only a matter of time before it came for you and everything that you loved. Eventually it would be your turn.

I vowed to never let anything like that happen to Lydia. I vowed never to let anything like that happen to any one of us. Still, I sensed the possibility.

We all did.

When I was four years old I had to go to a therapist because those Sally Struthers starving African commercials knocked me on my ass. The mere sight of the skeletal children with their sunken, hollow eyes was enough to level me. I may have only been in preschool, but my white-guilt was at a twelfth-grade level.

"Every year ten million third world children don't live

to see their first birthday," Sally would say, voice quivering as she toured the slums in an oversized purple blazer.

As she continued to lobby for these children across my television screen, I became more and more stricken. Eventually I took on their suffering. These kids were fucked from the get-go. Their chances of survival were nil. If they couldn't survive, I didn't see why I should. Never mind that they lived in Africa and I lived in Denver, Colorado. That wasn't the point. It wasn't fair. So I stopped eating, stopped drinking water. I began drawing fucked-up pictures of starving bodies, dead children on the ground with distended bellies. My parents were understandably concerned. They took me to a child psychologist, which eventually broke the spell. I don't remember much about the process, other than no part of me wanted to be there so I would just silently beat the shit out of one of those clown punching-dummies until it was time to leave. Eventually I didn't have to go anymore. It seemed I was cured. Africa, not so much.

Then I learned about Martin Luther King Jr. in kindergarten and the anguish took hold yet again. In anticipation of the coming holiday our teacher read us a book about boycotts and German shepherds and fire hoses and Selma and I literally wailed at the injustice. My parents had to be called. They did their best to ground the conflict that night, to highlight the progress made since then by so many heroes, which brokered a delicate peace. But every time I sniffed even a hint of discrimination I would break out into "We Shall Overcome," a little bowl-cut white child of the eighties crying as he belted out protest anthems at the top of his lungs. Had my teacher told us about Malcolm X, I would have stopped talking to white people all together.

The world affected me. Perhaps too deeply. How could it not? My father was a civil rights attorney; my mother was an investigative journalist. If you weren't outraged, you weren't paying attention. So you better channel that outrage to help fix things. That was the pervasive mind-set at Casa de Cayton-Holland anyway, one that my parents were proud of. Were we to produce a family crest it would be a picture of a child sobbing while he stabs the hegemon in the heart.

My father's father was an art dealer to the stars, a Beverly Hills sophisticate who dealt in everything from Dutch masters to Picasso. He was also a hard-ass who barely paid any attention to his kids. So my dad was left to his own devices in an iconic Los Angeles before the sprawl. His was a childhood full of baseball and avocados, high school classes with movie stars and Christmas caroling with Ricky Nelson. He could have easily gone into the family business, a rich kid turned rich adult, but the sixties lit a fire under his ass, and as a young man he reemerged a disciple of the civil rights movement. He wrote his college thesis on the legal rights of conscientious objectors across American history. After graduating from UCLA Law he joined Legal Aid, where his marching orders, as he loved to remind us, were to "do good, raise hell, change laws." He was assigned to Denver and left LA with his middle finger up; off to the Rocky Mountains with his long, black hippie hair blowing in the wind, off to raise some hell, do some good, change some motherfucking laws. Which is how he met my mom.

Linda Cayton was from the wrong side of the tracks, Richmond, Virginia. Poor white trash, she would say. Her father lied about his age so he could go off and fight in World War II at the age of sixteen. It fucked him up something fierce and he came back from the South Pacific drunk, abusive, and ready to start a family. He sobered up long before we were born, became a manager and father figure at a Richmond halfway home, but the damage was done. One heartbreaking story about my grandfather pissing on my mother's homework loomed large in her Southern Gothic. In spite of that, she got herself into Mary Washington College. The Vietnam War was raging and she quickly became radicalized and began writing for the student newspaper. She was having fun, burning her bra, sowing feminist seeds that would later manifest in the hyphenation of her children's last name, damning them to a lifetime of clerical confusion in the name of gender equality.

After college she snagged a gig with the College Press Service, a leftist group that operated as a sort of AP for student newspapers. They shipped her out to Denver. She filed hundreds of stories over the years and eventually began a series on the systemic corruption of nursing homes. Which was how she met my dad.

Criminally negligent behavior by nursing homes was

nothing new: they had operated virtually unregulated since their inception, unchecked warehouses for the sick and dying. But people like my mom were spreading awareness via the fourth estate, as was my dad through law. It was personal for him. His mother had been put in a nursing home when she was dying. On one visit he leaned in for a hug and came away with wet hands. Her back was one enormous, festering bedsore. It shaped my dad's career. Legally obliterating nursing homes became part of his life's work, a calling card. His evidence became part of the landscape of our youth. In the era before digital photography, getting the latest roll of pictures back from the grocery store photomat was a horrifying, high-stakes game of nostalgia.

There's Anna at the figure skating rink.

There's Adam playing soccer.

There's little Lydia on the piano.

BEDSORE! JESUS CHRIST! IT'S AS BIG AS A FIST! YOU CAN SEE THE BONE! THAT'S EVIDENCE! NEXT PICTURE!

We took it in stride. Without bedsores, we wouldn't exist. Bedsores put me through college.

When my dad met my mom he was working on one of the signature cases of his career, *Michael Patrick Smith v. Heckler*, a landmark decision that eventually led to the national Nursing Home Reform Act. My mom included the case in her series, so my dad called her up.

"You're going to win a Pulitzer if they don't kill you first," he said.

She liked the sound of his voice, found it authoritative and polished. She figured with a voice like that he had to be tall, dark, and handsome. He was a five-foot-eight Jew from Brentwood.

They had three kids. They wrote a clause in their will that said if any of those three kids puts them in a nursing home, none of us sees a dime. No bedsores for my mom and pop.

As take-charge as my parents were, they were also flower children of the sixties, overflowing with compassion and empathy. And that trickled down to us. Not only were we raised to rage against the injustices of the world, we were also taught to feel them deeply. For how could you possibly overcome injustice if you didn't truly understand it?

The suffering of the world crept into our fabric early, but for the most part it was theoretical. Something to be saddened by and fought against, but something we managed to avoid. Until my dad's best friend Wade Blank drowned attempting to save his son Lincoln—who also drowned—and the cruelty of the world took center stage. My parents had tried to protect us from it for as long as they could, but we learned that day that it was never really all that far away.

My dad met Wade on the Michael Patrick Smith case, the same one that led my mom to my dad. Wade was the whistle-blower at the nursing home; he fed my father intel about the abuse going on inside, my dad sued the shit out of everybody. They made a TV movie about it: *When You Remember Me*, starring Fred Savage and Ellen Burstyn. Wade was a disabled-rights crusader; he went on to found the disabled-rights group ATLANTIS and help pass the Americans with Disabilities Act. He was a hero. And then one day he was just gone.

Wade took his family to Mexico on vacation and eight-year-old Lincoln got sucked out into the deep by the vicious Baja undertow. Wade jumped in to save his son, but neither one of them made it out alive. All Wade's wife and daughter could do was stand there on the beach, watching.

I was twelve. Lydia was eight. We were deemed too young to go to the funeral so my parents dropped us off at a friend's house. But it made the local news and we watched that. There was a balloon release for Lincoln in the parking lot; we picked out my mom and Anna in the crowd. There was a shot of my dad behind a lectern delivering a eulogy. I put my hand on Lydia's back.

"You okay, Lee?" I asked, calling her by the nickname we all used. She and Lincoln were close, they played together all the time.

She didn't say a word. She just sat there, trembling.

What kind of a fucking world was this? What kind of higher power would ever allow this?

No kiddie shrink this go-round, but my dad—momentarily tabling his grief—removed a large book of photographs from the shelf to show us. It was full of images from the Hubble Telescope. We sat together and studied vibrant photographs of comets and quasars and stars exploding brilliantly in the heavens. My father explained that this was a world we barely understood. We don't know why any of it exists, he said, and yet here we were, getting to experience it. Getting to live in it, to marvel at the meaning and significance of it all. And how lucky were we to be able to do that, even if just for a brief moment in time?

We all reacted differently to the pain we felt. While I wailed and created bad art like a Hot Topic goth, Anna demanded answers and action, flexing her civil rights attorney muscles from an early age. She worked at ATLANTIS in high school and eventually served on the board, helping to continue Wade's legacy of fighting for social justice for people with disabilities. Lydia quietly ruminated. She suffered silently. Her teacher told us how she muttered to herself about Lincoln for months after his death, but would always deny it whenever someone pointed it out.

She never asked for help, or clarification; she just processed things on her own. Eventually she came away with this profound appreciation for all living things, no matter how small. Which only magnified the tragedy she saw and felt. There was human suffering and loss to be accounted for, but the same sad fate befell animals and insects, even plants. Lydia cataloged it all.

Our parents wanted to relandscape the front yard when we were young. Lydia wouldn't have it. She insisted that they had no right to rip plants out of the ground and murder them. Rather than ignoring her and going about fixing their front yard anyway, my parents honored Lydia's protest. Eventually they found a sympathetic gardener who offered Lydia a plea deal: he could take all the old plants and shrubs and trees and grind them into a mulch, which he would use to help fertilize a new front yard. That way all the old plants would be there right alongside the new. Appeased, Lydia allowed the landscaping job to proceed and our front yard boldly leapt out of the 1960s.

She became a vegetarian when she was nine.

Once we passed a dead animal on the side of the road and I noticed Lydia's lips moving, as though she were reciting a prayer. I called her on it.

"Are you praying, Lee?"

"No!" she insisted, repulsed. Religion was anathema in our house.

"Then what are you doing?"

"I'm saying, 'Rest in peace, little doodle.'"

Rest in peace, little doodle.

It was what Ned Flanders said to a cheese doodle in episode 89 of *The Simpsons*, "Boy-Scoutz 'n the Hood." After a disastrous scout trip, Homer and Ned and their sons find themselves stranded at sea in a raft, starving. Homer decides to use a cheese doodle, their last precious morsel of food, as bait to catch a fish. He ties it to a line, hurls it into the water, and despite everyone's protestations, he promptly catches a fish! Which promptly breaks the line and disappears into the water. Forever.

"Rest in peace, little doodle," Ned says sadly.

Lydia loved that line. She thought it was sweet. So in the absence of any religion growing up, she appropriated the *Simpsons*-ism as a shorthand eulogy for fallen innocents. I saw her do it on countless other occasions over the years, often unconsciously. Not one sad piece of roadkill escaped her attention, and always, even midsentence, she would stop and murmur those words like a silent reverie: *Rest in peace, little doodle.* Not only were all deaths wrenching for her, all deaths were also worthy of mourning. We traveled to Borneo and Indonesia when we were kids. Lydia cataloged every dead animal she saw the entire trip. The final tally was over a hundred. Many of them we never even saw. She sought them out.

Her vigilance was astounding. No death went unnoticed. She tried to cope as best she could, but you could tell that the death toll was adding up inside of her, like she was accruing it.

I found a poem she wrote when she was in the fourth grade.

There is a place in my heart reserved for two dogs,
    two special dogs that were here.
But this place in my heart is pierced by a tear, a
    very, very sad tear.
God took them for some extremely strange reason,
And I think of the time that they were still here as
    a great, special season.

Our dogs had been dead for two years at that point. The loss still felt fresh to her.

And yet, this was never a cause for alarm in my family. My parents expected their children to be smart and sensitive, they were proud we felt so enormously. We were the Magnificent Cayton-Hollands after all! If we were to become all that they hoped we could become, our hearts had to be open to the world—the good, the bad, the heartbreaking.

If there was ever any concern about mental illness, it would have been discussed. My parents sent me to a shrink at four; it was not a subject they shied away from. But this was the 1980s. The concept was hardly pervasive. Words like "anxiety disorder" and "bipolar" were still a generation away from commonplace. All we knew was that the world was a complex place, but we'd figure it out eventually.

Right?

The trick, then, became finding ways of circumventing the hurt and upset. If we were going to feel everything so damn acutely, we had to find a way to control those feelings instead of letting them control us.

Which is how we all developed crippling obsessive-compulsive disorder.

SECRET SUPERHEROES

It started with the tiny television in my bedroom, the one looming high on the dresser. Who knew what was going on inside that box? Starving African kids? Funeral of a friend on the local news? A rerun of Stephen King's *It?* Anything could be banging around those unilluminated tubes. Never mind that the TV was turned off. Inside there were some thirty-odd channels allowed to run wild while I slept mere feet away. My unconscious was susceptible to all manner of unchecked, osmotic horror.

So I developed a system for policing it. I would use the previous channel button on the remote control to leapfrog back and forth between Channel 4 and Channel 9 for seven couplets, before ultimately leaving it on Channel 4 and turning the television off.

04-09, 04-09, 04-09, 04-09, 04-09, 04-09, 04-09, 04.

Why Channel 4? Because I had done my recon; I knew nothing sinister was taking place behind the screen on that network. It was merely the local news, *The Tonight Show*, Tom Snyder, then paid programming and the rainbow stripes buzzing till dawn. Safe, innocuous content.

And if somehow over the course of the evening the television decided to meander of its own accord to oh, say, the last channel viewed, Channel 9 afforded a nearly identical viewing safety net. There would be none of the random slasher-flickery of Channel 31, no sci-fi befuddlement of Channels 2 or 9. The content was tame and antiseptic on Channels 4 and 9. So they alone were allowed to reign inside my television, their namesakes whispered like an *om mani padme hum* as the light fizzled inside the television and darkness swept over the room.

04-09, 04-09, 04-09, 04-09, 04-09, 04-09, 04-09, 04.

Next I had to make sure my pillow was perfectly centered in my bed, which I accomplished by gripping the outer bars of my wrought iron bed frame and then counting inward, alphabetically—A, B, C, D, E, F.

F was the bar where my hands met in the exact middle of the bed, and thus where I should place the center of the pillow. I would grip that bar with both hands over my head like a knight wielding his sword for a deathblow, and that was how I knew total balance had been achieved, and I could move on with my nightly routine.

Let us pray.

Dear Lord (we were agnostic), *Dear Lord, please bless Anna, Lydia, Mom, and Dad.* Then again, but in reverse, so that no family member would have preferential positioning over another: *please bless Dad, Mom, Lydia, and Anna.* Next, to the animals: *Please bless Lily and Tundra; please bless Mama Kitty and Baby Kitty; please bless*

Ramona, Sugar, and Amy. Please bless Sam the Turtle, and all of Lydia's rats. Extended family: *Please bless Grandma and Grandpa; please bless Uncle Lauren and Aunt Maynee and my cousins Molly and Griffin.*

Amen.

I then closed my eyes and hoped sleep would overtake me promptly. Because if it didn't I would have to get up and pee again, the tank needing to be absolutely 100 percent empty in order for proper slumber to be achieved. And then I'd have to start the whole process over again.

I don't remember when I started performing these nightly rituals. All I know is once I did nothing ever seemed to go to complete shit. Life as I knew it didn't collapse. And while I couldn't prove that this was strictly because of dogmatic adherence to my routine, I couldn't prove that it wasn't. In time it just became the truth: the world was a fragile place; my practices were the only thing holding everything together. Should I neglect my duties, who knew what horror would unfold? That's how the cracks opened. That's how the darkness crept in. It was an enormous burden, but it was one I was willing to bear. Because I was a secret superhero, the thin, neurotic line between order and chaos. I was unlike anyone else.

Except for the two girls living down the hall.

One day Anna confessed to me that before she closed her eyes at night the last thing she had to see was her bedroom door, *never* a window, or else terrible things would happen. My knees buckled.

My god. You . . . feel these things too?

Then Lydia revealed that she had to touch the door handle before the car was unlocked or she couldn't physically get inside, and I realized that all three of us shared this burden.

Once we learned of our shared compulsions, the floodgates opened. We traded our afflictions like Pogs. The rapid cataloging of teeth with the tongue, the depressing of diagonally corresponding bubbles on a to-go soda lid, speed-dialing to 100 on the telephone or a remote control, all of it helped. Nothing was too laborious or idiosyncratic. Our work was far too important.

Anna developed a nifty prerequisite for air travel wherein every member of the family had to meticulously study the emergency instructions laminate before taking off. Never mind our familiarity with the content, our cognizance of the sad little troll boy patiently waiting for his mother's assistance while she correctly attends to her own oxygen mask first. None of that mattered. This was a ritual and as such it had to be observed with diligence. Our parents obligingly studied the increasingly familiar bad clip art, heading off their children's panic attacks at the pass. For were we not to engage in these behaviors, who knew the devastation that would ensue? Planes might fall from the sky.

While Anna's and my rituals had been grand-scale, designed to avert the impending disasters of the day, Lydia paid homage to the god of small things. Hers became attempts to ensure the well-being of all. Should a food item fall and touch the ground, rendering it garbage, you can't just throw it away. Because then it will be lonely. You must throw another piece after it, another grape, another Goldfish cracker. Because then whatever sad fate those two food items are off to meet, at least they will be doing so together.

For Lydia, this extended to any inanimate object. A straw wrapper wasn't just bunched into a spit wad and thrown away. It was ripped into two, or three, or four pieces that were then discarded as a group, like some new gang of super friends off for the adventure of a lifetime.

It was Lydia in a nutshell: champion of the overlooked and miniscule; thoughtful, crazy, and kind.

We never asked for these burdens. They were bestowed upon us. And should we neglect them, there would be consequences. If not for the world at large, then for us personally. With great power comes great responsibility.

I knew this all too well from my migraines.

The first one was on my twelfth birthday. I had club soccer tryouts that day. I was in my bedroom gathering my shin guards and cleats when suddenly a flash went off behind my eyes somewhere deep. My temples felt like they were going to cave in on themselves. The pain was unbearable. I ran into the bathroom and vomited violently. Then I collapsed into my bed, writhing and grinding my teeth. My parents were beside themselves. What was happening?

I knew.

While countless doctors later would tell me the migraines

were stress-related, that the nerves of soccer tryouts sent me down that road, I knew it wasn't stress that had me groaning in agony. It was dereliction of duty. I had fucked up. I couldn't say for certain what I had missed: the list of rituals at that point was long and growing longer. But what did it matter? I had forgotten *something*. Why else would this be happening? Some unseen villain or vindictive god had uncovered my kryptonite.

It was the only justification I could think of.

Over the years, as the headaches came and went with ever-increasing randomness, I ignored the advice of professionals to shoot whatever new migraine drug was available up my nose. I heeded the only doctor's advice given to me that ever made sense.

"You have to calm your entire body down," one neurologist told me with didactic patience. "You start at your very tippy toes and say, 'My toes are at rest.' Then you move up to your feet and say, 'My feet are at rest.' Then on and on, all the way up until your entire body is calm and at peace."

Now here was a solution that made sense! A meticulous accounting of every single body part designed to summon order from chaos? The math checked out. This was the only logical remedy.

So as the migraines continued over the years, as the medicines and understanding of the phenomena supposedly improved, I ignored all the science. I took my cerebral lumps and adhered to my own, neurotic prescription. Sometimes it worked, sometimes it didn't. Sometimes I vomited multiple times from the pain; sometimes I saw spots so bad in front of my eyes I was unable to drive or read words on a page. But every time a migraine washed over me, I would retreat from wherever I was into the darkness of the nearest bedroom, lie there calmly and begin whispering to myself, "My toes are relaxed, my feet are relaxed, my ankles and Achilles tendons and shins are relaxed."

I would meticulously pull the wave of relaxation over my body, tracing the calm across every vertebra and rib, and as I did, a radiating peace would envelop me, a peace that somehow pierced through the pain, allowing me to finally fall asleep. It was like the turning point in every epic movie battle, that brilliant moment where you can feel the tide shifting away from the villain back toward the hero, toward the side of good, and right. Every time I drew the calm all the way up my body, finally coaxing it through the shaft of my neck and out through the top of my head, I would allow myself one final ritual, one last neurotic peace offering before collapsing into the darkness.

"Oh four oh nine," I would whisper with my eyes shut tight, tapping back into my essential binary code. "Oh four oh nine, oh four oh nine, oh four oh nine, oh four oh nine, oh four oh nine, oh four oh nine, oh four."

And like that, the world would be safe again.

But who knew for how long?

GHOSTS I'VE KNOWN

We were at the market on Kearney Street when the atmosphere suddenly swallowed itself. The temperature plunged, the sky turned eerie dark, a stillness enveloped the neighborhood. We quickly loaded the groceries into my mother's car, anticipating hellacious rain; then we heard the alarm. Children of the prairie states know it all too well: a disaster-howl that starts low and swells to a panic-inducing crescendo. The tornado siren. Growing up it rang every Wednesday at 11:00 a.m., a test of the emergency notification system that reverberated across the Mile High City. But it was just that. A test. Tornadoes didn't hit Denver. They happened out on the plains, damn near Nebraska. That was trailer park shit. We were city kids. We would hear that siren as we sat bored in our classrooms and we would giggle nervously and make stupid white-trash jokes; then it would subside and we would go back to staring out the window on a sunny day. But this was different. This was late in the afternoon, not on a Wednesday, and there was no sun. The sky was angry and alive. The clouds swirled, low and threatening.

We piled into our station wagon and my mom got the lead out, empty Diet Coke cans clanging loudly in the back with every high-speed turn. All around us neighbors were in disaster mode, racing their cars from their driveways to the garage, slamming their doors and windows shut. Ambulances and fire trucks tore past us in the opposite direction, deeper into Park Hill, our historic, tree-filled neighborhood. We turned onto Montview Boulevard, hauling ass, the odometer climbing to 50, 60, 70 miles per hour. Debris shot by. I looked in the rearview mirror and saw massive trees toppling some half-dozen blocks behind us, a chaotic melee of foliage and rain and howling wind. It was all so violent.

I caught eyes with Lydia. She was grinning, a fixed calm in the midst of the storm. She was frightened, but at the same time she was thrilled. Like she had been waiting for this, expecting it. *Here it is*, I could see her thinking. *Here is our tragedy.*

We didn't want to die, but a little taste of that damage would go a long way for our street cred. A little glimpse of the other side, the darkness. Like when you break your leg in school. No one wants to experience that pain, but then everyone signs your cast. Lydia and I longed for that that day, the way any American kid who seemingly has it all would. To not be in Kansas anymore.

We pulled into the alley and left the car parked in front of the garage. We burst into the house and my mom herded me and Lydia down the back staircase into the unfinished part of the basement, where there were no windows. She stationed us near the laundry room, among the boxes of extra Christmas decorations and old clothes, and then ran back up the stairs to retrieve the many animals that made up our household.

The neighborhood howled above us as we hunkered down together and waited out the storm. We tried to call my dad at work, to let him know we were okay, but the phone lines were down. The power was out in the whole neighborhood. Anna was in Colorado Springs at the time, staying with a friend for an ice skating tournament, so we knew she was safe; the radio said the storm didn't reach that far south. Other than that, everything was up in the air. We clutched our flashlights and pet the dogs to keep them from whining, and we prayed that the storm would spare us. Or maybe we prayed that it would bear down upon us. In our hushed reverence, it was hard to tell the difference. Lydia sat crisscross applesauce on the blue tile floor. Her eyes were dinner plates deep in her skull.

"I can't believe this is happening, Lee," I whispered.

"It's incredible," she said.

We waited, our hearts in our throats. Anything seemed possible. Everything seemed possible. The true nature of the world, maybe of ourselves, was revealing itself.

And then, suddenly, it was all over. Outside grew quiet. The storm subsided and we headed back upstairs.

Our portion of the neighborhood had been spared. The tornado hadn't made it that far west. But it had touched down in east Park Hill, knocking down enormous old trees into several houses, collapsing power and telephone lines. City workers moved in quickly to address gas leaks.

When the phone lines were back up we touched base with my dad and let him know we were alive. That mom had gotten us home safe. She had saved us. We checked on friends and neighbors and for the most part everything was all right. Some damage to property here and there, but no fatalities, just a scare.

All that hype for nothing.

That night my dad told us how during the worst part of the storm everyone in his office building got on the roof and watched the tornado touch down in Park Hill. He said looking out across Capitol Hill, then City Park, you could actually see the funnel cloud form and drop from the sky. He explained how it would touch the earth, then immediately recoil, almost timidly, before working its confidence back up, pouncing again. He told us how frightened he was, how helpless he felt as he stood on the roof and watched a tornado terrorize *his* neighborhood, where his wife and son and daughter were, and with whom he couldn't communicate. He was overcome with emotion. He hugged us and kept us close to him all night. I wondered if my father suspected something like that might happen all along. Like we did.

"We were hoping it came closer!" I blurted out.

"Why would you want that?" he demanded.

"I don't know," I stammered, suddenly aware of how

spoiled it was to pine for a disaster. "Just to, like, see it better. Right, Lee?"

She wisely kept her mouth shut. I was flailing.

"Well that's ridiculous," my dad said. "You should be grateful nothing bad happened."

He was right. We were lucky. Still, when I think about that period of our lives it's easy to remember Lydia like that: desperate for something else, something dark and familiar, a mesmerized child staring through the back windshield into the chaos of a howling storm.

SIGNATURE BITS

We weren't raised religious; eighties sitcoms became our doctrine. The Huxtables on the staircase lip-syncing to "Night Time Is the Right Time?" A character actually named Boner Stabone? Carlton doing the Carlton Dance? This was our gospel. Here were all the answers, here were moments of sheer joy, of unthinking, in-the-moment Zen. We couldn't get enough. We devoured it wholesale, re-enacted it, riffed off of it. Right there in the basement, on that patch of carpet that would eventually become so worn it would need to be replaced, we developed our sense of humor.

We ran bits.

Especially Lydia and me. Because while Anna was off pursuing figure skating at early morning and afternoon practices, we were down in that basement letting the TV colonize the far-flung recesses of our brains. Lydia continued her studies when Anna got home; the two often binged *Star Trek* together deep into the night. But at that point I would take my leave. Space was for nerds. Comedy was all I needed.

One Friday evening, as was often the case, Lydia and I found ourselves parked in front of the TV devouring ABC's TGIF slate. *Thank Goodness It's Funny.* We'd gotten to *Full House*, the crown jewel of the block, and we were watching like jack-o-lanterns as Michelle Tanner was learning to play the recorder. She was trying to plow her way through "Bah Bah Black Sheep" but every time she got to a certain point in the song, the recorder would play a flat note. She just couldn't get past it. No matter what she did differently, same flat note, every damn time. So Uncle Joey gave it a try. Same result. He looked in the recorder and realized there was an obstruction. So he blew into it as hard as he could, and a wad of bubble gum shot out and hit Michelle directly between the eyes.

THWAP.

Lydia exploded. It hit her just right. She laughed so hard she couldn't breathe. Then suddenly she let out this deep, troubling wheeze, a shocking sound that made us both laugh even harder. It sounded like Robert Carradine's laugh in *Revenge of the Nerds*. It was disturbing, like a sickly clap at the end of a coughing jag. We shared one of those tears-streaming-down-your-face, *I'm-gonna-pee, I'm-gonna-pee* types of laughs.

"What the hell was that, Lee?!" I asked her.

"I have no idea!" she said. "I didn't mean to do it!"

"Can you do it again?!"

"Maybe!"

After a few attempts, she found that she could, and we

burst out laughing anew, just as hard as the first time. We were both so delighted that tiny Lydia could ever produce such a sound that we pursued it full tilt. With a little more practice Lydia was able to do it three times in a row, and with a little more tinkering, she was able to make the noise *while* saying the word "Hi," much to our insane delight. We fashioned this new bat-shit skill into a character and ran with it. She became a lonely foreign exchange student, Margo, a young girl oh so eager to please, but who, alas, only knew two American words, "Hi" and "Bye." Poor Margo, all she ever wanted, all she so desperately longed for in this strange, foreign land was to fit in, to be accepted. But damn if that cursed sound didn't scare away all her peers!

"Hey Margo," I would start. "Some of us kids were going to go ride bikes. You want to come?"

Her eyes would widen, she would smile deliriously and began quivering with excitement, like a Sarah McLachlan kennel dog finally shown a moment of attention.

"Hi!" she would belch, a TB patient escaped from the sanatorium.

"Um, excuse me?" I would continue, face contorting into a disgusted sneer.

Beside herself, she would belch out another series of disturbing yelps, frantically waving hello the whole time, desperately imploring this new friend not to leave.

"HI! HI! HI!"

I would feign disgust, totally weirded out.

"Uh . . . like, never mind, Margo," I would say. "What is wrong with you?"

Then Margo, tragic Margo, would go back to her sad little corner of the world alone; she would tuck her knees into her chest and let out one more defeated, disconcerting, bark.

"Bye . . ."

And then, poor Margo would die. And we would roll around on the carpet in hysterics.

What can I say? We were very alt.

Soon Lydia discovered that she could speak backwards. Fluently. The trick was that she had to be able to spell the words she was saying. If she could picture the letters in her head, she could flip them, read them, and then spit them back out instantaneously. That's just how her brain worked. That fast. Lydia could read the world backwards as easily as she could forwards. Both versions made sense to her. We didn't know why. We hypothesized it was from when she was a toddler and shoved a magnetized, travel-sized checker so far up her nose that my parents didn't discover it for two days, when the stink could no longer be ignored. But we didn't question it all that much. All we knew was that it was an amazing parlor trick we could use. So of course we gave the skill-set to Margo, adding more and more nuance to our beloved character like *SNL* scribes desperately trying to get Lorne to make the sketch into a movie. Eventually, Margo would belch her strange hello, then, once rejected, she would mutter to herself inconsolably in her backwards language, sounding like some wretched, Eastern European wench.

We performed the act in front of my parents. Though initially alarmed, they quickly lost their minds laughing. They wiped the tears streaming from their eyes. Who were these weird fucking children?

We were always running new bits, playing new characters. Like this pair of hick siblings ever threatening to tell on one another for whatever backwoods atrocity they'd committed that day.

You don't gimme your Mountain Dew I'ma tell Daddy how you tied all them kids to them trees!

You do that I'll tell Daddy you mutilated them squirrels!

Tree-tied kids way worse than mutilated squirrels!

Sometimes in carpool one of us would start sounding off about the bad lunch meat we'd tucked into that day at school, feigning queasy and begging whatever poor bastard had driving duty that afternoon not to swerve so much. The bit would quickly escalate from groans to full-on retching. This, naturally, would trigger the queasiness of the other, who had also horsed down said dubious deli meat, until eventually both of us were holding our stomachs and fake-puking from the backseat as loudly as we could. Whoever was driving would yell at us to stop but we'd stick to it with such conviction that eventually they would succumb to our routine, transitioning from yelling at us for being annoying to yelling at us to stop so they didn't lose control of the wheel from laughter. Either that or the bit would just tank completely. We were about 50/50. But we didn't care. We were making each other laugh, and that was all that mattered to us. It became how we related; every conversation between Lydia and I would quickly veer off into absurdity. We felt comfortable there, safe from looming danger. It seemed more fun to laugh at the world then to cry about it.

Summers we took our road show to City Park, the crown jewel of the city. It was a mere three blocks from our house growing up. Any iconic shot of Denver you've seen, it's taken from there: the lake, the boathouse, the downtown skyline, then the foothills rolling up into the mountains. Postcard City Park. And once we were old enough to cross busy Colorado Boulevard on our own, it was all ours.

My mother was a volunteer docent at the Denver Zoo, right in the center of the park. She worked in the primate house. She often helped raise rejected apes and monkeys until they were healthy and old enough to reintroduce back into their enclosures. But they'd still pine for their caretakers. So my sisters and I would walk the zoo hand-in-hand with our mother in her beige vest with the green name tag and visit all her little friends. Katie the capuchin who made kissy-lips at my mom; Bungee the spider monkey who'd loved my mom and would come running toward her screaming, fully erect. We would laugh so hard people must have thought us simple.

They named Katie's baby after my little sister: Lydia the capuchin.

Eventually my mom began working in the nursery, and sometimes, if the nice vet techs were working, we'd get to help feed whatever baby animal was currently housed there. You never knew what you were going to get. An artic fox baby. An African wild dog. America's polar bear baby sweethearts Klondike and Snow. We got to meet them all.

It felt like we were celebs, in on this secret that the general public never got to see: a busy world of carts darting every direction and animals pacing in the backs of their enclosures. We'd make our way through the nurseries' offices, then the enormous kitchen, down the narrow corridor with the off-exhibit crates and cages and then into the main nursery, the one with the display window out to the public. Passing zoo-goers would watch jealously through the glass as an army of baby mongooses crawled all over us or a golden lion tamarin baby nursed a bottle in our arms. The envy on the faces of the schoolchildren passing beneath us was palpable.

Why do those kids get to do that and we don't? Why are they so lucky?

Because we were born into it. We live here. This park, this zoo, this is all ours. This is our home.

And isn't it amazing?

We were also members of the Natural History Museum, which sat next to the zoo. Entire days were swallowed there. Days of the Hall of Life and the sloths in the tar pits and the mineral caves and the plastic saber-toothed tiger that roared when you put a coin in its mouth. But our favorite were the animal dioramas. Floor after floor of them, from all over the world: Africa, South America, Australia, the Antarctic. We knew each continent backwards and forwards.

And we knew about the gnomes.

One of the original muralists painted them there as his calling card: tiny little gnomes that he would hide somewhere in his landscapes. If you didn't know to look for them they were nearly impossible to find. They were perfectly camouflaged in the background. But they were there just the same, as a reward for those who knew to seek them, tiny little treasures to hunt for across multiple floors of taxidermy. A museum employee told us about them and over the years we found every last one. And nothing delighted us more than pointing them out to unsuspecting visitors. We'd stand in front of a diorama and wait for a new group of visitors to approach, then launch into our favorite bit, a clumsy shill.

"Say, what are you looking at?" Lydia would ask me, loudly, the audience plant to my carnie shuckster.

"You don't see it?!" I'd respond, incredulous. "There's a gnome hidden in the painting here!"

"There is?!" she'd reply, flabbergasted. "Where? I don't see it."

Then I'd loudly explain to her exactly where it was located.

"See that big tree, the one next to the rock? Look on the right side of it, one, two, three branches up. Beneath that branch, in the background, crouched in the river, there's a gnome!"

"Oh my god I see it! That is so cool!"

"Right?"

Inevitably people would want in, and after our ruse we were perfectly positioned to bask in the admiration of strangers. They were always so tickled and delighted once they finally found them. As were we. The bit had worked. Two-fold. Not only had we shown them the secret of the museum, but in doing so, we had made ourselves special. Like we were somehow different, with an enhanced understanding of the world. Our world. The zoo, the museum, City Park, Park Hill, Denver. It made us feel bigger than ourselves, like we were connected to some greater plane, one where the treasures of the world were at our fingertips. We wanted everyone to realize that there was mystery and wonder right there in our backyard if they only knew to look for it. There was so much more beneath the surface.

A CAREER IN THE ARTS

The public schools in my neighborhood were shit so I had to go Graland Country Day School, a neo-Fascist lacrosse factory in the form of a K–9, a place so pretentious it actually existed in a neighborhood called Hilltop. At Graland the progeny of emotionally distant businessmen and their manic-depressive trophy wives gathered on a daily basis to perfect their pronunciation of the word "faggot" while sowing the seeds of future opiate addictions.

One fall—fifth, maybe sixth grade—flag football became popular at recess. But rather than a gang of kids picking sides and hurling the ole synthetic rubber around, teams were formed. Soon contracts were negotiated, actual documents were drawn up on college-ruled paper and signed. Promises were made and fulfilled: a donut in the morning once a week to play for a certain squad, a soda pop every day at lunch for a speedy receiver to jump franchises. Flag football became a business. Once money began changing hands the administration shut down the league. That was Graland: a place where children didn't want to be football players, they wanted to be owners.

I grew up on the wrong side of Sixth Avenue from Graland Country Day School. Though my neighborhood of Park Hill was decidedly upper middle class, at least on the south side, it was treated as the lefty ghetto to their Country Club right. I was never out-and-out bullied because I was good at sports—my flag football contract was a king-sized Twix on Fridays—but I was different there, an outsider, a quiet weirdo from the wrong neighborhood. Until one fateful morning in the ninth grade.

On Fridays every student in the upper school—grades seven through nine—was required to attend a weekly assembly. And at the end of every assembly, a different ninth-grade student was made to deliver a two-minute speech on the subject of their choosing. The administration figured it would behoove the FBLA Hitler Youth to get some public speaking under their belts. Ninth graders lived in perpetual fear of their turn at the podium. Every week we would watch some poor bastard sheepishly make their way to the front of the room and try to climb inside of themselves over the course of two painful minutes. They'd stare directly into the ground or sweat profusely; they would pause awkwardly and stutter, choking out disconnected thoughts about riding horses or skiing. The ninth-grade speeches were so unilaterally terrifying that they were off-limits from standard ridicule. What was the point? We all had to do them. There was no separating one speech from the other; they were all nightmares, another humiliating ordeal in a long string of humiliating ordeals that, cobbled together, somehow constituted an Ivy League admissions package.

But for me, those ninth-grade speeches were an opportunity, two golden minutes when the entire upper school *had* to pay attention to me. I didn't intend to let it go to waste.

Dave Letterman was my own personal Jesus at the time. I had negotiated my bedtime to after the Top Ten List, which allowed me to watch Dave's opening monologue, whatever bat-shit opening sketch the writer's room had concocted that evening, then the Top Ten List. The Top Tens were my favorite—so dry, so precise, so joyously and deliberately odd. So when it came time for me to speak in front of the upper school, I decided this was my opportunity to write my own.

Graland underwent a massive renovation that year, a seemingly endless construction job that left an enormous hole in the middle of school. They walled off the crater so we wouldn't topple into it, but it still loomed there mysteriously, noisy and dusty, like a meteor crash site in the middle of our otherwise pristine campus.

So I wrote a Top Ten about it.

I took to the podium, all thirteen years, four feet eleven inches of me, and cleared my throat.

"It's time for tonight's Top Ten!"

Tonight! It was 8:00 a.m.! The irreverence! The entire audience immediately perked up.

"Top Ten Things the School Plans to Do with That Giant Hole in the Middle of Campus."

I removed a note card from my pocket on which I had written my Top Ten and proceeded to tick them off, one after another. And it fucking destroyed. Crushed. Showtime at the Apollo, the little rich, white asshole version. People couldn't believe what was happening. It was unlike anything they had seen all school year. This was not some painful experience to be omitted from our collective memory. This was noteworthy! This was *funny*. I savored every second. I ad-libbed and shook my head in delighted disappointment at the joke, just like Dave. I watched the waves of laughter roll over the audience, waited for them to subside, and then hit them with the next joke. It was the single most electric moment of my childhood up until that point.

And it was over all too soon.

The headmaster clapped me on the back and retook the podium.

"Now *that* is how you do it!" he said to the entire upper school. "Nice job, young man."

The effect was immediate and overwhelming. I was the buzz of the campus.

Did you hear that Adam read a Top Ten List at the assembly?

That kid who stands in the hallway counting lockers all the time?

The very same! And it was hilarious!

Everyone wanted to be my friend that day, funny by association. I soaked the attention up greedily. I knew that it would vanish all too soon, but I didn't care. This was my moment and I was going to bask in it. I sat at a completely different table in the cafeteria that day, apart from the early-acne adopters with whom I usually dined. Fuck 'em. They didn't exist that day. Girls who had never spoken to me in the many years we'd been in school together fawned. One stopped me and asked if I was Adam Cayton-Holland.

I was.

She immediately dropped to her knees and sucked my dick right there in the hallway. Okay, not really. But the high I felt was as if she had! I was someone different that day. Someone of note. I had done something that none of them could do. I had been funny. Gotten up in front of a room and gotten laughs. And it had opened doors, instantaneously blown them right off their hinges!

It all went away the next day. Of course.

Baby boy, you only funky as your last cut
You focus on the past, your ass'll be a 'has-what'
—André 3000

My Top Ten was forgotten like a dream by the entire class. No one said a word about it. Things went back to normal. I was an outsider again, completely ignored. Back to the loser table. Back to obscurity. That's just how things were for me at Graland. But though the school remained the same, I was different. Something changed in me that day. Something irrevocable. There was before that day, and then there was after. Now began the after. A fire had been lit somewhere deep inside me. This whole humor thing might just be the ticket.

A career in the arts was born.

AMBASSADOR OF HOPE

One Sunday afternoon my freshman year of college I awoke from a three-day booze- and pot- and coke-filled bender, desperately needing to piss. I started down the hallway toward the coed bathrooms, then hit the floor. I opened my eyes moments later to my hysterical RA telling someone to call an ambulance.

"No, no, no," I stammered, knowing the trouble I would get into if someone were to run any sort of diagnostic on me in the moment.

"Your face is green!" she shouted.

"I'm fine! I'm fine!"

She was meek, a sweet Canadian in need of the financial assistance she got for being an RA. She was not equipped to handle this shit. I pushed her out of the way and hurled myself into the bathroom, where I promptly passed out again in front of the sinks, green face on cold tile. More hysteria, more screaming, more false assurances on my part. I headed back down the hallway to my room and slammed the door behind me. I slept it off for another six hours and emerged relatively intact. But everyone looked

at me differently on the hall after that. People saw a darkness in me.

I had followed Anna to Wesleyan University, in Connecticut, and while she looked after me the best she could,
brought me extra slices from her shifts at Giuseppe's Pizza
like a good older sis, she was also busy with her junior year.
I didn't want to bother her. And truthfully, I was ashamed
of how badly I was doing. Within two weeks of getting to
college I had been cut from the soccer team and rejected
by the newspaper. My identity and confidence vanished. I
did not rise to the occasion. I sunk. My face exploded with
acne. I grew remote and insecure. I made friends with the
kids that partied way too hard and I drank and did more
drugs than I ever had in my life up to that point. I needed
help but I didn't want to let on—to Anna, to Lydia, to my
parents, to anyone. I felt like they expected better of me
and I didn't want to disappoint them. I couldn't shake the
feeling like I wasn't doing college right.

Weren't these supposed to be the best years of my life?

My mom used to tell a story about her days as the co-
editor of her college paper. *Roe v. Wade* had recently made
abortion legal, but because of a legislative oversight it was
still illegal to advertise for abortion clinics. The Virginia
commonwealth attorney let it be known that if any liberal student newspapers decided to test him on the matter,
there would be hell to pay. So a coalition of student editors
agreed to all run ads for clinics in their respective papers
on the same day. They figured he couldn't prosecute them

all. Then the fateful day came around and only my mom and her co-editor followed through. They were summoned to the commonwealth attorney's office. They sent a car for them and everything.

"We'll need you to pull the ad immediately and print an apology," he told my mother.

"Or what?" she said, all firebrand redhead.

"Or I'll have you arrested," he responded, certain that would settle the matter.

They told him to go right ahead.

The good-ole-boy attorney clucked, flustered. He was stuck between an abortion and a hard place.

"Well, I would never have young ladies arrested," he stammered. "Just don't do it again."

They left his office and continued to run ads every week, completely undeterred. My mom said she never heard another word from the commonwealth attorney again.

That was how my mom tackled Mary Washington University. My seminal collegiate moment thus far had been discovering how good Red Bull tastes in a forty.

I was not living up to my potential.

In high school, I was my mother's rightful heir apparent. As editor in chief of the school newspaper I spearheaded a humor edition that got the entire staff into all kinds of shit—then won awards. I was the funny guy, the provocative writer. I graduated number three in the class, I was a star soccer player. I was someone.

That Adam Cayton-Holland, keep your eye on that one.

I felt loved and supported and respected there, and now, at Wesleyan, I was no one. There were a thousand kids like me. And two thousand far more impressive. These were East Coast elites, from fancy boarding schools up and down New England and progressive preparatory schools in Manhattan. They had saddlebags and wore peacoats. They were driven and sophisticated and blossoming while I withered. Lin-Manuel Miranda was in my class. Nobody looked in my direction and saw a *Hamilton*. Nobody looked in my direction at all.

I felt small and insignificant and far away from home. And it was all-consuming. I fought the darkness off as best I could but I just sank deeper and deeper.

People used to say that the dorm I lived in my sopho-more year of college was haunted, that there was a ghost in Hewitt Hall. The details were unclear, but the general consensus was that sometime, awhile back, a student had taken his life there and now that same unfortunate soul haunted the dormitory. People claimed they saw things: the figure of a young man behind you as you brushed your teeth in the mirror, an apparition that always vanished when you turned around to investigate. Some reported hearing loud crashes at the end of the hall, garbage cans being hurled about. One student swore that every time she went into the coed bathrooms a faucet would inexplicably turn off and on by itself. They were popular ghost stories people told one another as fall turned to winter and New England turned gray and claustrophobic. But I never saw or heard anything. And I haunted that dorm far more than any ghost.

I couldn't sleep for days on end. I'd spend grueling hours lying on my extra-long twin mattress, tracing the arc of the moon across the sky, unable to turn my brain off. Eventually I'd grow so frustrated that I would get up from my bed, dress, and leave my room. I'd walk around the dorm, daring the ghost to show himself, lingering for long spells at his purported haunts, traipsing silently through the hallways. But he never appeared.

Sometimes I'd sit at the top of Foss Hill in the middle of campus and think about being back home, some two thousand miles away. Sometimes I'd go for long jogs through the wooded area that surrounds the school. Mostly I'd go to the nearby Indian Hills cemetery and wander among the old mausoleums and crumbling headstones.

I'd think about killing myself.

I had a number of ways that I wanted to do it. Most of them involved overdosing. Might as well have one great final trip on the way out. The violent stuff I couldn't go in for. Slitting your wrists. Shooting yourself. What if it went wrong? How painful. Though hanging myself also appealed to me for some reason. Something so poetic, no blood, no gore, just a swinging silhouette of a man who couldn't take it anymore. Of someone who had enough. There'd be no doubt who haunted Hewitt then.

I'd think about who would come to my funeral, who would remember me, who would forget. I'd wonder what they would say about me, what my legacy would be. All the sad, shitty stories and poems I was writing—they'd certainly have more meaning once I killed myself. Maybe someone would publish them.

They'd notice me then.

But I was too big of a coward to ever pull it off. I just thought about it all the time, about becoming the ghost I spent so many nights chasing.

Except for when I was vandalizing. The darkness I was fighting off, the depression, all of that drifted away when a long night of binge-drinking was allowed to culminate in its inevitable conclusion of me breaking shit. I felt free in those moments. I felt a reprieve. Never mind the fact that I was some asshole nineteen-year-old nihilist howling at the moon, some self-obsessed liberal arts school prick ruining it for everybody else. None of that mattered then. I didn't care what anyone else thought. That was the point. I was able to shut my brain off and mute all the dark thoughts that plagued me every other second of the day.

Call it Zen.

I liked everything about vandalism. The sound of the glass breaking, the risk of getting caught, the endorphin release, all of it. I felt alive. It got me high. I was always the last one to run off. We'd destroy something or hurl a fire extinguisher five stories down the center of a stairwell and my friends would yell after me to get out of there, that we were going to get caught. But I lingered as long as I could, soaking it all in, laughing. I was listening to too much Pink Floyd at the time; I felt like it spoke specifically to me.

Hey you, out there beyond the wall breaking bottles in the hall, can you help me?

I couldn't. I couldn't even help myself.

Walking home drunk from a party one night, a buddy and I kicked over a trash can. A passing group of girls noticed our idiocy.

"Ooh, some real bad boys," they teased. "You won't knock over that other trash can."

Trash can down.

"What a bunch of badasses," one of them said. "You guys are too cool for us."

They walked off, totally oblivious to what they had started. I had tasted blood. No mere trash can would pacify me. We wandered past College Row, a tier of iconic, stone buildings in the dead center of campus. They were renovating the old '92 Theater. It was an active construction site zoned off with yellow tape. I ducked under the tape and found a metal rod lying on the ground. I jumped into the chair of a parked bulldozer and began smashing the control panel to pieces, a wild animal. My friend yelled at me to stop but I was too far gone. I was possessed by a darkness. I was spinning out of control. This was my cry for help, I was going to see it through.

I leapt off the bulldozer and, wielding my new weapon with two hands over my head, I hurled the metal rod through the enormous window of one of the neighboring brick buildings. Direct hit. Glass poured down from above, a purifying shower that cut my face, hands, and legs. Sweet release.

I was instantly seized by the strong arms of a mammoth Public Safety officer. He had heard the breaking of the glass of the bulldozer and snuck up on me. Within seconds five Public Safety cars were there, lights flashing, all of them full of screaming officers.

"What's your problem with the president of the university?" they demanded.

"I don't have any problem with him," I responded, confused as to why they were asking me that. "The food here sucks."

"Then why did you break his office window?" they yelled.

"That was *the president's* window?"

Much later, I would play up the fact that it was the president of the university's office window. It seemed cooler that way, like I was a rebel making some sort of statement. That sad truth was that I had no idea whose window I was breaking. I just aimed for a patch of glass and threw.

The next morning, the head of Public Safety knocked on my door with an incident report.

"Fill this out by this afternoon," he said, disgusted. "We'll initiate the proceedings after you do."

I consulted with an older vandal I knew, a senior with some disciplinary experience under his belt.

"The trick is to make them laugh," he told me from his perch on a futon festooned with dirty laundry.

"Make them laugh?"

"Absolutely," he said. "You're going to have to go in front of the student advisory board. They see all kinds of dumb bullshit every week. They get bored. If you can get a laugh from them just off your incident report, they'll be on your side already. Then they'll go much easier on you."

His logic seemed sound. Throughout my life, humor was the glimmer of hope, the place I felt most at home. The most powerful. I could do this. So I filled out my report.

To whom it may concern: last night while trying to emulate a move from the movie "Braveheart" I attempted to hurl a metal rod with two hands over my head against a wall. Unfortunately, my aim was not as good as Mel Gibson's (hey, whose amongst us is?) and my shot went dreadfully awry, shattering the president's window in the process. I apologize for any inconvenience and hope they will be able to fix the window soon.

They skipped the student advisory board all together. I was placed on immediate "interim suspension," meaning I was barred from campus, despite the fact that there were two more weeks in the semester. I was forced to move into the off-campus house of several sympathetic hockey goons and had to send friends to the campus center to retrieve my meals. Were I to be caught on school grounds at any time, I would be immediately expelled. So I stayed out of sight; there but not there. Like a ghost.

Fortunately, I had Anna on my side. Unlike myself, Anna was well liked at Wesleyan, involved in numerous school organizations and on several administrative committees. She was on a first-name basis with many of the deans we would be dealing with. She took up my case like the powerhouse attorney she was born to be. We sat through a half-dozen meetings, and every time Anna calmly and patiently painted my actions as a cry for help, help that I would be taking proactive measures toward getting. She argued that the university was overreacting in the wake of a yearlong wave of vandalism, none of which they could prove was my doing outside of the night in question. She reminded the deans that in these moments they had the opportunity to showcase what a school like Wesleyan was all about. Was it a place that turned its back on its students when they were most in need, or was it, as she liked to believe, a place that helped the most vulnerable members of its community when they were in trouble?

Somewhere in the middle of a deposition a shiver must have shot up my father's spine.

Anna's measured approach sprung me. Over the course of her stalwart representation, talk of immediate expulsion dwindled to nullifying the semester, which shrunk to suspension, which finally gave way to two years of probation, paying for all of the damage, one hundred hours of community service, and mandatory psychological counseling for "rage." It didn't hurt that I would be studying abroad in Spain the next semester, and would not physically be on campus for eight months. I was, for all intents and purposes, a free man.

Somewhere toward the end of that fucked-up semester, toward the end of what had been up to that point the worst year of my life, Lydia came to visit. And everything slowed down. The world stopped moving so fast and played out in real time, at a pace I could understand. Things recalibrated and made sense again. Oh yeah. Lydia. My other sister, the little one, a lifeline from a previous existence, one where I felt grounded and safe. She came like a messenger from a past that was far more me than whatever it was I was becoming. She was fifteen, a curious high schooler on her first visit to a college campus. Anna and I took turns hosting Lydia for a couple of days, showing her our school, and all the other bullshit went away. There was no depression then, no thoughts of suicide. It was just the three Cayton-Holland children on the far side of the country, away from our parents, together.

Two years earlier I had been in the exact same boat, off to Connecticut to see my big sis. I was filled with excitement and anticipation. The whole world was out there in front of me. The formative years were fading into the past, it was all right now, and everything beyond. Life felt like it was finally beginning. I knew Lydia was feeling that way too and I didn't want to burst her bubble. I didn't want her to see what I had become since I left home. I didn't want to be so lost. Not in front of her.

She had dyed a thick, blue streak in her hair at the time.

That was a total surprise to me in an era before social media. My little sister, the punk rocker. I asked her if she smoked weed and when she told me that she did, I proceeded to take her to a party and get her higher than she'd ever been in her life, an elder sibling's responsibility. When we left that party Lydia told me that she could see the people moving their lips but she couldn't hear a single word anyone was saying. We smoked some more and laughed and laughed and laughed.

She had an early morning flight the day she left. I'd prepared a little pallet on the floor of my dorm room for her; a nest of blankets and comforters and pillows. Neither one of us could sleep, so eventually we just gave up. I climbed down into the floor fort with her and we watched movies all night together. We giggled, ran new bits. It felt like old times. Then the sun was rising and it was time for my little sister to go. I had an early class, so Anna drove her to the airport. Lydia waved at me as they drove off, looking back at me through the rear windshield, like we had at that tornado all those years ago. I can still see them driving away together, my sisters. I wasn't a ghost in their eyes; I was one of them. It wasn't okay to just disappear.

I had a test that day. After Lydia left I trudged off to class and realized that I had not studied at all. I sat down next to a friend of mine who asked me if I was prepared. When I told her I wasn't, she told me I could just cheat off of her. She angled her test toward me. I sat there for a moment, debating, and then I just gave up. Fuck it. I put my pencil down, slid the exam away from me, and left. I might be a nobody at that school; I might be depressed, suicidal, stalking the campus at night like a goddamn madman, but at the very least I was no cheater.

Not that I was a zealot against cheating. I didn't take the school's solemn proclamations about the sanctity of the honor code to heart. I was engaged in all manor of depraved behavior on a regular basis, who was I to judge someone for cheating? But Lydia's visit reminded me of who I actually was.

Leaving the test that day, in a way, began the long and convoluted road to pulling myself out of my depression. There would be more vandalism and drugs and alcohol, but pushing that test away and heading back to my dorm room for a few hours of so desperately needed sleep was the first act of many in making myself better. Of remembering the decent person at the core of myself. Of choosing to live.

And Anna gave me that.

Lydia gave me that.

I wish I could have returned the favor.

PIRATES AT THE EQUATOR

" 'It's been insane,' said an exhausted Cayton-Holland.' "

That was Lydia's quote in the *Denver Post*. A big, bold pull quote, smack-dab in the center of the article. It was 2004. Dubya was running for his second term and the media was stoking the fears of the 2000 voting fiasco on a near-daily basis. Some intrepid reporter wrote an article about the perils of absentee voting—new twist on an old fave—and they somehow tracked down Lydia, who was studying abroad in Ecuador, apparently mired in difficulty fulfilling her civic duty.

"It's been insane," said an exhausted Cayton-Holland.

That was the entirety of her contribution to the article, which just about killed us. It was my family's favorite inside joke for months after its publication. We regularly parroted her response, adding a surfer accent for effect like some sort of patriotic Jeff Spicoli.

"How's law school going?" my mom would ask Anna.

"It's been *insane*, said an exhausted Cayton-Holland!" Anna's response.

And while that quote was merely a favorite tidbit from

Lydia's time abroad, a shorthand anecdote we could use when people asked how she was doing, there was also something reductive in our affinity for it. We knew that was merely the quote the reporter chose to use; there was an entire interview beyond that. We also knew that Lydia was no platitude-spouting imp, that she was perhaps the smartest of all three of us, capable of rallying an entire voting bloc of expats should the need arise. But it also wasn't hard for us to view Lydia in the way she came across in the article: exasperated, flustered, overwhelmed.

There was an air of *welcome-to-the-big-leagues-kid* in our enjoyment of that quote. Lydia was the baby, the tag-along, the third of three. It was always easy for her to just sit back and enjoy the ride. She was gifted in many different realms—piano, breaking down *Buffy the Vampire Slayer* with doctorate-level precision—but practical matters often eluded her. She once drove fifty miles on a toll road without stopping, only realizing the error of her ways when the massive bill arrived at my parents' front door. And here she was, a foreigner in a foreign land—it wasn't hard for us to imagine her as out of her depths. As a fish-out-of-water for whom every simple turn proved harrowing. Or *insane*. Perhaps we found that quote so funny because subconsciously we had expected it.

Who then, was the woman that greeted us at our hotel in Quito, after we flew halfway down the world to meet her? Not the child my parents had said goodbye to at the airport, not my little sister Lee, but this actual, elegant grown woman. She was wearing a flowing dress—*Does Lydia wear dresses?* She wore her hair down to her ass—*Had Lydia ever worn her hair that long?* She had cool earrings and bracelets, a beautiful, handmade necklace—*Did any of you buy Lydia those things? I don't remember buying her those things.*

She seemed transformed. And not falsely so. She was grown up all of a sudden, totally at home in her skin. For a perennially awkward skinny girl, beautiful but atypically so, with a nose like a Cubist painting, that really meant something. Lydia preferred the shadows, yet here she was at center stage, seemingly seizing the moment. She appeared before us not as the baby of the clan, but as a full-fledged member, claiming the position that was so rightfully hers.

Lydia showed our family around her little study-abroad corner of the world over the next few days—Anna and I pining for our similar experiences in Paris and Madrid, my parents pining for the time when they didn't have to pay for everything. We kept looking for cracks in Lydia's veneer, but we couldn't find them. It was legit. At every turn we were amazed by her transformation.

Over dinner one night her new friends explained that not only was Lydia the funny one of the group, she was also "the leader." Here was a title no one had ever bestowed upon my little sister. Lydia was a seeker of the broken, a gatherer of misfits perhaps, but she did so with the sheepish uncertainty of any outsider. *Leader* was a stretch. Yet there she was, splitting the bill for eight student budgets; mother-henning drunk friends into cabs, barking their addresses to each different driver.

At a salsa bar one night Lydia casually related to Anna and me the story of her mugging. She was walking through a part of town known as Gringolandia, between her host family's apartment and the university where she was taking classes. The conventional wisdom was that the area was fine to traverse by daylight, but to be avoided after dark. Of course that conventional wisdom didn't necessarily hold up for a tiny white girl from the States. Which is how Lydia found herself being robbed at knifepoint in broad daylight, a stream of pedestrian passersby just looking the other way.

The mugger demanded she give him all her money. Lydia said of course. But she kept her wallet in the saddlebag straddling her torso, so she awkwardly began rotating the satchel from back to front so she could reach into it. Which wasn't fast enough for her assailant. Agitated, the prick demanded she just hand over the whole bag. At which point Lydia patiently explained, in Spanish, that the bag was a recent gift and that she really loved it; if it was all the same to him, could she please just fish out the money and keep the bag? As well as the other few items in there she was fond of?

The mugger was so taken aback by the request that he quickly acquiesced. The notion of rolling a gringa for some easy money was one thing; having a conversation with a fluent expat was another. Suddenly he felt embarrassed by the whole exchange. After Lydia spoke up, he could no longer hold eye contact; he kept apologizing and calling her "senorita." He was polite and deferential. By the time she got her wallet out Lydia felt so in charge she actually had the mugger hold her saddlebag while she removed the cash from it. She handed him the cash, he returned her bag, and they both went along their separate ways in Quito.

To hear Lydia tell it, the whole experience was really quite pleasant.

Who was this woman in my little sister's body?

I distinctly remember thinking on that trip that she was going to be just fine. That she was finally beginning to realize her potential.

The whole family left Quito after a few days and boarded a plane bound for the Galapagos. We spent five days bouncing from island to island. We saw finches and albatross. We saw cormorants that had evolved so that they were no longer able to fly. We hugged giant tortoises, sized up frigates and boobies, both red-footed and blue. And when we weren't doing that we were shit-talking the elderly Germans and Brits that brazenly colonized every corner of our eco-cruise.

Conservatively I would estimate that my sisters and I were eighty-five years younger than the youngest among them, and as we politely moved aside so they could waddle down one of the ship's many narrow corridors, we silently cursed them for either killing the Jews directly, or being too weak to prevent it.

We ignored our shipmates from the Continent and

instead hung out with the crew, who loved us. Our age alone would have made us favorites. The fact that all three of us spoke Spanish made us virtual ship celebrities, our every move well documented.

"You swim with a sea lion today, eh?" the man slicing the meat would say to me at dinner with a wink.

"I did!"

"Eso es!" he would exclaim, delighted, piling an extra portion of roast beef onto my plate.

Lydia and I riffed constantly on that trip. We knew that "abogado" was Spanish for "lawyer," but we didn't know that South American attorneys also flaunt their doctorates in their job title. We learned this walking through Quito one day, when we stumbled upon a block of law offices, each one proudly flying the sign "DOCTOR ABOGADO."

Doctor Lawyer.

Anna was about to graduate law school and begin work at my dad's firm. We begged her to announce herself to the Colorado legal community at large as Doctor Lawyer. It would not only set her apart from the pack, we insisted, but lend her an air of worldly sophistication. She declined. Didn't matter. Doctor Abogado was born; he became our go-to supervillain, his name only spoken as though he were a dastardly fiend.

"So we meet again, *Doctor Abogado*" Lydia would vamp. "Did you really think you could brazenly keep filing slip-and-fall after slip-and-fall and the court would simply fail to take notice?"

"Tell me, *Doctor Abogado*," I'd yes-and. "Did you actually listen to your Continuing Legal Education Seminar tapes, or DID YOU JUST SAY YOU LISTENED TO THEM?!"

One afternoon, Eddie, the ship's point man, pulled my sisters and me aside, all business. He explained to us that the ship had a long and storied tradition for when the vessel actually crosses over the equator. While the guests are out on the deck enjoying their afternoon cocktails, some of the crew dress as pirates and run around pretending the ship is under siege. Eddie explained that normally such a privilege was the exclusive domain of the most senior crew members, but because they liked us three so much, they were hoping we would take the reins.

Eddie, I thought, *this is a terrible tradition*. A cheese-dick sketch for a bunch of septuagenarians who normally reserve laughter as a means of shaking crumbs from their folds? No thank you.

"We'll do it!" Anna said.

"Really?" Eddie asked, delighted.

"Absolutely!" Lydia chimed in. "We would be so honored."

Eddie beamed, then ran to tell the others.

"We're not really going to do this, right?" I protested.

Anna gave me the type of look that only a family member can muster, a look that says not only are you going to cease your line of questioning immediately, you're going to back the fuck up and proceed in the opposite direction entirely, regaling all who you encounter with the story of how foolish you once were. I turned to Lydia for reinforcement. She stared back at me with the exact same look.

"Quit being such a baby," she said.

Treachery on the high seas. Lydia was my go-to comedy collaborator. Not only did we share a sense of humor, but also a sense of mortification. And self-respect. We were never the drama geeks hyperventilating at their own hilarity as one of their bits plays out in front of the food court. We were the cynical assholes watching those neckbeards and mocking them. Yet here we were staring down the barrel of a total comedy fucking disaster and Lydia's only response was to start an improv troupe. All we needed was a fat guy in a sweater.

An hour later we were sitting in a cabin off the main deck preparing for the show. A crew member helped us don wigs and eye patches and ill-fitting pirate garb. Eddie handed us a page-long script he had printed out. It called for three pirates and a Poseidon. As if on cue, my father, the original *Doctor Abogado*, bounded into the room wearing a tight-fitting gold tunic, the fanciest of sausages. He had a long, white wig on and he clasped a plastic trident in his hand. He was smiling like a special needs student.

"I'm Poseidon!" my father loudly announced, unable to contain his joy.

Our improv troupe was complete.

My mother, for her part, wisely sat out the performance, opting to drink chardonnay and write postcards in her cabin instead, dignity intact.

As we neared the equator, we peered through a window toward the unsuspecting European lizard-people, warming their massive carcasses with goblets of gin. They had no idea they were about to be bitch-slapped by a four-man, dinner-theater flash mob. Then Lydia spoke up, inspired.

"We should just swear as much as possible."

"Swear?" my dad asked her. "Why?"

"Because fuck it. We're pirates. Pirates swear."

The logic tracked.

"WE'RE CROSSING THE FUCKING EQUA-TOR!!!" I bellowed, belting out of the cabin, plastic swords flailing. "AARGH!!!"

"YOU HEAR THAT, SHIT-BAGS?!" Lydia screamed. "WE'RE CROSSING THE EQUATOR!"

"WHICH MEANS YOU BETTER FUCKING PAY ATTENTION!!!" Anna joined. "AARGH!!!"

As the script called for, we each grabbed a stunned spectator and dragged them to the front of the deck, where we forced them to get on their knees. The crowd was rapt.

"Ladies and gentleman!" Lydia yelled. "All hail King Poseidon!"

The audience applauded and my father emerged like a resplendent, silver-haired drag-queen: Too Wong Jew.

"Who dares cross the equator without consulting me first?" he demanded of the assembled mass. "I am Poseidon! I must be satisfied!"

He was *owning* it.

"AARGH!" Anna gargled, herding an old English man

she had plucked from the crowd toward my dad. "FUCK-ING TAKE THIS ONE!"

The man shuffled toward him, blinking and uncertain.

"You!" King Poseidon continued, angrily, absolutely stealing the fourth-grade spring play. "You've been flushing toilet paper down the toilets when the signs blatantly say to dispose of all paper products in the trash can!"

"WHAT THE SHIT, MAN?!" I screamed.

"YOU KNOW IT'S A DELICATE SEPTIC TANK!" Lydia echoed. "ARE YOU STUPID OR JUST AN ASS-HOLE?"

"For your punishment, you must do the mating dance of the blue-footed booby!" my father ordered.

Relieved that this was the extent of his punishment, the timid Brit shuffled in place, doing his best imitation of a ritual we had all seen so many times over the last few days. The crowd roared with approval. The crew handed him a fancy pink drink, and the Brit promptly disappeared below deck like a mole who'd been above surface far too long.

It went on like this for what felt like forever, though I can't be sure. Time has a way of eluding you at the equator. The three of us would round up fat Europeans and swear at them, my father, King Poseidon, would dole out punishments, the bar would reward everyone with silly drinks.

Finally, we reached the end of the script.

"Ladies and gentleman," Lydia said. "A round of applause for King Poseidon!"

My father bowed humbly, holding on to his wig like an

ace, lest the whole cover be blown. Then he regally made his way back to the cabin.

"And remember," Lydia cautioned, beginning to lose her voice from all the pirating. "REDUCE!"

"REUSE!" Anna followed.

"FUCKING RECYCLE!" I screamed.

We exited. Hysteria reigned. We'd crushed.

Back in the small cabin off the deck, we caught our breath and removed our costumes and makeup. Eddie promptly joined us and positively shrieked with glee. He said it was hands down the best equator crossing they'd ever had. He thanked us profusely and gave us each a king-sized Nestlé Crunch bar, a rare commodity so far out at sea. Then he left us alone to come down from our performer's high. We tucked into our candy bars with ravenous appetites, three pirates and a King Poseidon, feasting together on their hard-earned bounty. Then Lydia spoke up.

"It's been insane said an exhausted Cayton-Holland."

We all laughed. Lydia smiled. The joke was no longer on her.

JESUS IN A TORTILLA

I was at a bar waiting for a friend when I struck up a conversation with the man seated next to me, the way two heterosexual males never do. I had graduated from college and was back in Denver, trying to figure out my next move. The year was 2004. The bar was the Red Room. The man was Ben Roy. I'm surprised there's no commemorative plaque.

Here Asshole A met Asshole B and together they went on to create extended cable glory.

Ben had tattoos covering seemingly every inch of available skin and was scribbling away in a small notebook.

"Are you a writer?" I asked him.

"No," he said, definitively. "I'm a comic."

Never mind the fact that he had been doing stand-up comedy a paltry six months at the time. In Ben's mind, he *was* a comic. That was good enough for him.

"Are you a writer?" he asked me.

"Yeah," I said, trying to sound cool. "I write for *Westword*."

Never mind the fact that by that point I had had one essay and three upcoming event blurbs published in my hometown alt-weekly. Never mind that I was substitute teaching to actually pay the bills while struggling to get pieces into the paper. In my mind, I *was* a writer. That was good enough for me.

Two young Skywalkers. The delusion was strong in these ones.

Ben and I chatted more as we waited for our respective friends. I peppered him with questions about stand-up comedy, fascinated. I had never met an actual stand-up. Up until that point I didn't think that they walked among us. I thought they only existed in blazers in front of brick walls, anointed on high by the Late Night gods. I didn't think it was something you could just do. I was never one of those guys who fixated on stand-up as a kid. Colorado cable packages didn't even offer Comedy Central until late into my teenage years. And what little I did know of comedy, I found lame. Dudes with mullets bitching about airplanes. Uncle Joey on *Star Search*. But here was this punk rock dude talking about stand-up with an intensity I found mesmerizing. You could tell he lived and breathed it. For him stand-up was as valid as any art form out there, if not more so. Because there was nowhere to hide, as Ben explained. It's just you and a microphone. And what's a purer form of expression than that?

Our respective friends arrived, but before we parted ways that night, Ben told me about a dive bar down the street that hosted a comedy open mic on Monday nights.

"It's called the Lion's Lair," he said. "You should check it out."

The next Monday I was there, saddled up to the bar alongside a handful of career alcoholics. The open mic was supposed to start at ten. It was ten thirty. No sign of comedy anywhere. Just a bartender who wordlessly slammed your drink down in front of you and a *Galaga* machine that hadn't worked since 1981. The windows were so thick with show posters you couldn't see outside, and the effect was suffocating, like a black hole. This was the place where all things vanished. In time I would come to love the bar for just that: a dingy refuge where the only thing that mattered was what was going on inside those very walls. That night, it just felt like somewhere I shouldn't be. I nursed my beer and stared at a velvet painting of a topless brunette wondering if I had made a mistake. Then a skinny guy in a baseball cap walked through the door and the room came alive. He started the jukebox up, got himself a Miller High Life, and began setting up the mic stand while fucking with everyone within earshot: Troy Baxley, local legend, unapologetic weirdo of the night. One by one comics began trickling in, signing up with Troy. After another half hour we were off and running.

Troy was phenomenal. So odd, so completely comfortable in his own skin. His material felt like those bizarre private gags you have with close friends, strange premises and scenarios capable of sending you into hysterics, but bits that sounded stupid when you tried to explain them to anyone else. Except with Troy they didn't sound stupid. They were hilarious. He was telling inside jokes and yet somehow everyone was in on them. It reminded me of how I riffed with Lydia.

I watched a cavalcade of comics take the mic and while there were a handful of truly funny ones—including Ben Roy—what struck me was how awful most of the comics were. How awkward and nervous and not funny. It made my skin itch. Who were these sad people? Where did they come from, and why were they doing this to themselves? What oversupportive peer group had allowed them to think this was something they were ever capable of? What middle school bullies dropped the ball? I watched three comics have good sets that night, and watched twelve others eat shit. I left that evening sure of one thing: I was way funnier than most of those assholes.

The next Monday I was back with jokes, terrified. I sat at the bar nervously sucking down PBRs. I had memorized my material so as not to appear amateurish but I was worried I was going to forget everything so I kept running it in my head, over and over, mouthing the words like a street-fanatic stuck on a particular psalm. I thought about leaving several times. Finally, Troy tapped me on the shoulder, snapping me out of my reverie.

"You're up next," he said. "Try to keep it to four minutes."

There was no turning back now.

The comic before me limped to the finish and Troy took the mic. "This next comic is what open mic night is all about!" Troy said. "It's this guy's first time onstage, so be nice. It's fun to kick a puppy but it's *just wrong*."

I slinked up to the stage, took the microphone out of the stand, and promptly blacked the fuck out. It was a legitimate out-of-body experience. I remember feeling the heat of the lights on my face. I know that time passed. I know that I shared some lame observations about having a hyphenated last name, closed with a bit about how every actor reaches a point in their career where they feel they have to play a mentally disabled person, but I only know that because I had memorized the bits. I wasn't conscious of performing them. It was like I had time traveled. The black hole of the Lion's Lair swallowed me and spat me out four long minutes later. And in this new future I was putting the microphone back into the stand while the audience laughed and applauded.

I felt like I had seen Jesus in a tortilla.

It was so immediate. So thrilling. I wanted more. I wanted back on that stage. I was like the kid who gets off the roller coaster then immediately sprints to get back in line. Or maybe I was like a junkie, feening for that next little taste of attention, of approval. I didn't know what I was. And I didn't care. I just knew I wanted that feeling forever.

"That was your first time?" Troy asked me into the mic as I exited stage. "Christ, man! Great job!"

I became something new that night on Colfax, Denver's famed boulevard of broken dreams. I became part of something bigger than myself. As comic after comic took the stage after me, I inhaled drinks in a dazed euphoria, shit-eating grin tattooed across my baby-face. This was what I had been looking for. The humor writing in high school and college, the shitty screenplays and poetry and short stories, it was all leading up to this moment, this feeling. And all of it paled in comparison.

Some of the other comics complimented my set; they told me about other open mics I should check out, told me I should call down to the Comedy Works downtown and sign up for New Talent Night. Suddenly this entire new world was opening up to me. The week previous I had watched a couple of other first-timers eat shit onstage, then watched as they were promptly shunned by the regulars at the mic. And yet here I was, being welcomed into the fold. Not the most exclusive club in the world, but laughter was the price of entry. And I had gotten laughs. Like that, I was a stand-up comic. I was born again. I never sought out to become a comedian. I just became one.

I was twenty-three.

In my experience, stand-up comedy either takes hold of you completely, or it doesn't. I've seen many a performer so initially possessed by the comedy demon fizzle out after a couple of months, their passion for the craft exorcised by the realities of the profession. But for me there was no turning back. The first time I told jokes on a stage I knew I would continue to do so for the rest of my life. It was a full-on conversion.

I continued along the path toward writer. I got a full-time gig at *Westword*, campaigned my way into a weekly humor column called "What's So Funny." I wrote cover stories where I shadowed gypsy cab drivers and mom-and-pop burrito peddlers; I smoked cigarettes with the food editor and music critic in the alley and bitched about all the transplants ruining our city. I was never not asking questions. I played the part of journalist. But it was all a front. I was just killing time until I could do comedy. I was paying the bills through my day job so I could come to life at night.

Comedy Works was the real prize, the vaunted stage looming on the horizon of my comedy future, so close you could taste it. It was the holy grail of the Denver comedy scene, the place where I would sneak in on weekends to watch Dave Chappelle and Greg Giraldo and Bill Burr, the place where I could have my mind blown watching the modern masters. It was where professional comedy actually happened, every night of the week, and I wanted nothing more than to join its storied ranks. But that was still way in my future. You didn't just *get* on that stage. You had to earn it. You had to grind it out for free, for years. Us rookies weren't even allowed to flirt with that stage, except for New Talent Night on Tuesdays. But that wasn't enough. So my buddy Greg Baumhauer started another open mic at the Squire Lounge, just down the street from the Lion's Lair. And we got to work.

The Squire was truly depraved. It opened at 9:00 a.m. It reeked of Jim Beam and vomit; the doors were ripped off all the bathroom stalls. Fruit flies were endemic. I once saw the drunk-tank *drop a guy off* at the Squire. Vagabond alcoholics frequented the place with whatever money they could scrounge up: $1.25 a draft, a buck provided they didn't start any trouble. Which was never the case. Not a night went by that some drunk asshole wasn't eighty-sixed for trying to start a fight with a broken bottle or grabbing some girl's ass or puking in one of the ripped-up pleather booths. It was disgusting, but we loved it. The juke was good, the bartenders had senses of humor, and the PA system sort of worked. It was perfect.

The tenor of Greg's open mic matched the surroundings in which it was born. Or maybe it matched Greg. Hard to say. Chicken/egg kind of thing. Greg was one of us, a Lion's Lair standout with a filthy sense of humor. The bluer the better. He had the most sordid past—full of horrific teenage-runaway tales, and his weekend gig as a drag queen waitress at the Bump & Grind kept him flush with ridiculous anecdotes. Greg's style of comedy was shock and awe, and the Squire took on his persona. It was ruthless, cruel, and unusual. Greg quickly christened the place "The Meanest Mic in America," and he made sure that tone was set comic after comic. Bomb onstage? Greg would rip you apart after. Kill up there? Greg would rip you apart. One had to mine the muck just to stay afloat. Fortunately, we were more than up to the task.

Every week we found new ways of grabbing eyes and ears, typically through the crassest means possible, the riskier the better. Incest, AIDS, abortion, eating disorders, suicide—we joked about them freely, unfortunate forays made by many an open-micer who fashion themselves edgy, eager to test the boundaries and see what they're able to get away with. Were we to come up ten years later, in 2014 as opposed to 2004, we would have been HuffPo'd into shamed silence. A bunch of foul-mouthed white guys perpetuating the patriarchy. As it was, no one was paying attention. We were young comics far from Chicago or Los Angeles or New York, far from any industry or opportunity besides the promise of one-nighters in Wyoming and Utah, so we howled lewd jokes into the void on Tuesday nights to an audience on welfare. We were developing our own signature, throat-grabbing Denver comedy sound, one born out of necessity, a style that assumed indifference and responded with preemptive aggression.

Call it middle-kid comedy.

It would have been easy for us to stop there, to rest on our dick-joke laurels and become career bar comics, because yelling "Where my drinkers at?!" always worked and who wanted to work all that hard anyway? But a miraculous thing happened there at the Squire Lounge on Tuesday nights. We did. We wanted to work that hard. Because we wanted more. Whether we were bored with cheap sensationalism or we were just reaching the next inevitable stages of that elusive comedy concept of *finding your voice*, one by one, we all started turning corners. The Squire made us all deft in the various ways we would grab an audience's attention, but soon we were able to hold it. With jokes. Well-written, good jokes. It seemed every week we would trade off winning the $25 bar tab handed out for the best comic of the evening: Ben Kronberg, myself, the various pros like Chuck Roy and Louis Johnson who would drop in to see what the young bucks were up to. We started sharpening one another. And we started getting really competitive.

Though Greg started the Squire as a place where we could do whatever we wanted onstage in relative obscurity, with little risk of failure, soon it became a show we took as seriously as any showcase or Comedy Works set, and soon enough, so did other people. Greg christened his little empire Wrist Deep Productions, and that became the unfortunate moniker under which we all labored, at the Squire and beyond. Greg and I started putting on shows constantly, wherever we could. But the Squire remained our favorite. Word about the wild, free, funny time was getting out, and after a little while, actual comedy fans began showing up: musicians and hipsters and cute girls and cynical dudes eager to get drunk for cheap and laugh. For every crackhead tweaking at the corner of the bar by the porno match-game, there were three newbies there for the comedy. Newspapers began writing about the Squire's comedy night. The bar would go from completely dead at nine to one-in, one-out by ten. Suddenly our little shit show was a hot spot. We had a real winner on our hands.

It was time for something more.

At work the music editor had thrown one of the many promotional CDs he got in the mail on my desk. It was a double CD called *Invite Them Up*, a compilation of some of the best performances from the beloved NYC indie-comedy fixture hosted by Eugene Mirman and Bobby Tisdale. I gave it a listen and had one of those clichéd movie moments where the younger brother has his lid flipped by Zeppelin or Pink Floyd or the Who or whatever album he stole from his older brother. You know the scene I'm talking about. The kid puts the vinyl on the turntable in his bedroom, places the massive earphones over his cool seventies haircut, then lies down on his bed with his eyes closed and is taken away to that special place, where everything else drifts away.

Like that, but with comedy.

I slid that CD into my work computer, popped my earbuds in, and I nearly fell out of my rolling chair. I listened to Demetri Martin and Mike Birbiglia, I inhaled hilarious, nonsense sketches by Michael Showalter and David Wain, and I laughed so hard my coworkers grew concerned. It was so weird and free and dumb, and yet at the same time, hyperintelligent. *This*, I thought. *This is exactly what I want to try and do.*

Los Comicos Super Hilariosos was my attempt.

I recruited Andrew Orvedahl and we set out to make the show unique from any other show in town, not just stand-up, but sketches and videos. A real comedy experience. Our first show culminated in a sketch that involved suits, theme music, a PowerPoint presentation, KFC Bowls, and a defibrillator. We were swinging for the fences. The eleven people in attendance—mostly my older sister Anna and her friends—loved it. But the next month there were twenty people there. Then forty-five. Soon we outgrew the place and the boyfriend of a coworker invited us to come perform at his art gallery down on Larimer Street. So we moved over to the Orange Cat, where things really took off.

Something about the space complemented our show perfectly. It was rough, but beautiful. Obscure, but ambitious. Walking down the desolate streets of a Denver that doesn't exist anymore, audience members wondered if they had the right address. Then they opened the door into the beautiful turn-of-the-century space, with its exposed brick and fading, hand-painted ads from when it was once a grocer, and they were immediately proud of themselves for knowing about something so cool. The Orange Cat was like you were in on a secret. And for one night a month we were that secret. It became our comedy clubhouse. The proprietor, Sean, turned over the keys and let us pop in at all hours to rehearse, to set up elaborate gimmicks long before the show started. I brought on Greg Baumhauer and added Jim Hickox, who was hilarious and knew how to make videos. Ben Roy eventually folded into the mix. We pooled all our meager fan bases and people began showing up in droves. Our efforts coincided nicely with the national rise of alt-comedy as a coveted cultural source, the phenomenon of podcasts and "Lazy Sunday" and comics gaining credibility with appearances on *Wait Wait* . . .

Don't Tell Me! In Denver, we were the faces of that, the alt kids. We began selling out every month, lines literally around the block.

"If comedy is the new punk-rock, Wrist Deep is the new Black Flag," the *Denver Post* gushed.

We practically jerked off to that quote.

We put on Los Comicos Super Hilariosos for four years straight, Denver's reliable alt-comedy fix the last Friday of every month. And when we weren't thinking about the show we were expanding our own comedy horizons. We were no dummies. We knew that however loudly we were howling in Denver, we were howling into a relative void. The big markets were in LA and New York. So we hit them as hard as we could. We worked our connections, got on the best shows that would have us and tried to get noticed, to stand out. Ben Roy punched his way into the New Faces at the Just for Laughs comedy festival in Montreal, an honor akin to being drafted by the comedy world at large. He was on the radar.

I opened for Tig Notaro and she was gracious enough to invite me to a comedy festival she was putting on in Washington, DC. I did well enough there to score an invite to the Bridgetown Comedy Festival in Portland, Oregon, the mecca of alt-comedy at the time. Which led to invites to perform at cool shows in LA and New York. Which I followed up on. I saved up money and days off from work and started making trips to New York and LA regularly. Eventually I got a manager in LA. I was staring to get noticed. He told me that there would come a time when I would have to move to LA, and he'd let me know when he thought that time was, but for now it was totally cool to stay in Denver and keep doing what I was doing.

I was more than happy to. I was always looking to shift the comedy spotlight back home, we all were. We loved what we had going on. We invited every funny comic we encountered to come perform on our monthly Los Comicos baby, or reached out to them when they were passing through Denver for other shows. Los Comicos hosted Tig Notaro, Maria Bamford, Greg Proops, Moshe Kasher, the Sklar Brothers, Natasha Leggero, Arj Barker, Kyle Kinane, many, many others. We became the show you *had* to do if you were passing through town, this little off-the-beaten-path gem.

Meanwhile we were climbing the local ranks, fast. From the time Los Comicos started to the time it ended, myself, Ben, and Andrew all went from open-micers to headliners at Comedy Works. We became big dogs in the Denver comedy scene. Troy Baxley, our hero who hosted the Lion's Lair, was *asking us* for time on Los Comicos. We had become big fishes in a small pond, but we were desperate for more water. We were ready to do comedy for a living. Fuck day jobs, just comedy. The dream started to seem achievable.

GUITAR HERO
GRANDE DAME

Sometimes I wonder how differently things would have gone if Lydia had never come home from Ecuador. She was thriving there; she seemed so content and healthy, so sane. What if she had just stayed? Sometimes I indulge my fantasy fully. I imagine that she's decamped from the big city of Quito to Cuenca, a high-mountain, colonial gem. She's married a little indigenous man with a mustache. He makes hats. He loves her and treats her well. They have fresh fruit on their kitchen table and Guayasamín prints on their walls. They eat lots of quinoa. They have a couple of kids who speak this weird hybrid of English and Spanish and Quechua. It's hilarious on its own, but Lydia's taught them all to speak backwards too, just like she was able to. They sound like adorable little aliens. They do it easily, of course; they all have nimble minds, just like their mom, the beautiful woman from America. So they speak backwards whenever she asks them to and they don't mind doing it because it means they get to see their mom come unglued, every single time. They perform for her and she lights up and laughs and laughs. They get to see their mother experience such pure joy. She loves them so much.

Or what if we had just let her be down in Colorado Springs? How much better would things have turned out for Lydia if we had left her alone after she graduated from Colorado College? Never pushed her. Never prodded. She seemed to be happy living in her college town those few years afterward; why was that not enough? She worked at a no-kill pit bull shelter. Volunteer of the year, two years in a row. Fêted at a banquet and all that. She had a boyfriend who helped run the punk club in town, the Black Sheep. My parents helped her buy a little house in a cute neighborhood down the street from the Colorado School for the Deaf and the Blind. She fostered dogs and cats and musicians and outcasts. Her friends all loved her. They seemed to orbit around her. She was this five-foot-five, late-night *Guitar Hero* party grande dame.

What was so wrong with that?

Nothing. But Lydia was a Magnificent Cayton-Holland. And we expected more.

Our family was never one for pressure, some Waspy vultures out of J. D. Salinger sneering at their progeny's every errant move. If you asked either one of my parents what they wanted their children to be, their answer, unequivocally, would be *happy*. And they would mean it. Had we sniffed at the cracks forming beneath Lydia's surface I don't think we would have pushed her, not even subliminally. But we didn't know. We never negated anything she was doing, but we encouraged her in various directions, the way you would any smart young person you care about making lateral move after lateral move in their early twenties. You step in and offer guidance and advice. That's the way of the world. Ours anyway.

She was so good with animals, why not think about vet school? The animal shelter was a great résumé builder for such an endeavor, surely she didn't want to make less than minimum wage with no health insurance forever, right? Colorado State University is one of the best vet schools in the west. Maybe she could go there?

Or at the Black Sheep, why not jump into a band? Lydia was gifted at piano and guitar and drums; she was spending night after night at the punk club helping bar-back anyway, why not play a little music?

But Lydia always had some excuse. Vet schools were inhumane. She didn't want to have to do that much dissection. And if she became a vet, she would never be able to handle putting down any animals. It would break her. And while she was good in the privacy of her own home playing all those instruments, she'd fall apart up onstage. She wasn't a rock star. She was a hobby musician. Nothing more.

Excuses, excuses.

They may have been no more than the meanderings of any twentysomething, but there was an insistence about them that was infuriating. The way Lydia seemed to tether herself to this career mediocrity. You could argue with her until you were blue in the face, there was no hurdling her reasoning. She was so stubborn.

Which was exasperating. Lydia was brilliant, plain and simple. She was so heightened, so fiercely precise. But it was always masked by a casual aloofness. She had this nonchalant intensity about her that you could miss out on completely if you weren't paying attention. She would let slip the most insightful comments in sly asides, half-uttered quips. The effect broke many a sad-bastard singer-songwriter into ten thousand terrible lyrics. She was special. And she knew that. She was also smart enough to see that her older sister was a civil rights attorney and her brother was this comic/writer while she was hosing dog shit off of concrete and killing drunks with kindness in a dingy punk club. So what was the problem?

I wonder if some part of her knew that fucking up was a way for her to stand out. We all glorified and fetishized dark books and movies and TV shows. What's more of an attention grabber than the kid who comes home for Thanksgiving strung out on drugs? And while Lydia was not there—yet—I think part of her knew that the best way to stand apart in a group of cocky navel-gazers who all fashion themselves exceptional was to be normal.

I often wonder if I steered Lydia toward comedy when I should have just left her alone.

I had gone down to visit her for the day in Colorado Springs. She drove me around to her favorite haunts:

Shuga's to eat, the Leechpit for records, the Black Sheep to meet the gang. She took me to the shelter where she worked and introduced me to Dozer, a massive pit bull rescued from an underground fighting ring. He was so far gone when he came in they thought they were going to have to euthanize him. He was traumatized and ferocious; he lunged at anyone who came near him. Lydia was the only one able to break through. Over months she rehabilitated him completely, and now he was this total sweetheart, this enormous shelter mascot, ready for adoption, waiting on a good home. All because of my little sister. We walked Dozer down by the creek behind the shelter, off an office park in a sketchy part of town. Lydia explained that according to the police who had briefed the shelter recently, that creek was where nearly half of all rapes in Colorado Springs took place. She delivered this tidbit upbeat, classic Lydia smart-ass. Like, wasn't that great news! I stared at my tiny sister, aghast.

"Jesus, Lydia."

"I'm fine," she said, showing me her cat-ear self-defense key chain. "Besides, I never walk down here without Dozer. He'd *destroy* anyone that tried to touch me."

"You should move back to Denver, Lee," I told her. "Colorado Springs fucking sucks."

"Believe me," she said. "I know."

That encouraged me. That she was souring on the Springs. It was time to come back to Denver, to her family. It seemed so dumb to me that she was just an hour away, living this separate life from her family. She had tons of friends in Denver. She wasn't doing anything in the Springs that she couldn't do in Denver. Besides rehabilitating pit bulls, which are archaically banned in Denver, a subject on which Lydia could opine for hours.

We saw the remake of *3:10 to Yuma* and when it was done, neither one of us wanted to stop hanging out. We missed each other. I had a gig that night in Castle Rock, a cluster of McMansions halfway between Denver and Colorado Springs, so I invited Lydia to join. She got someone to cover her shift at the Black Sheep and we caravanned north on I-25 to the gig. She had seen me perform several times—indeed, she had organized shows for me and my friends at the Black Sheep—but it had been awhile. And I had gotten a lot better. I was headlining showcase shows now. I was semi in-demand.

The show that night took place in a strip mall coffee shop where a Pier 1 Imports appeared to have projectile vomited all over the walls. They served no booze and there was no stage, just a mic stand on the floor. The setting was far from ideal but the room was packed. There was an audience there for the taking. Unfortunately, none of the comics seemed up to the task. I watched as the openers got up and meekly performed to tepid indifference. But I'd be damned if that was going to be my fate that evening. My little sister was in the house. I was Adam Cayton-Holland, of Squire fame. Of Los Comicos Super Hilariosos! Apathy was my fucking gasoline. These golf course polyps didn't know what was about to hit them. I took the stage and howled into that microphone. I refused to take *meh* for an answer. I went into the crowd and interviewed people, desperately wrangling. And it worked because that type of hacky shit always works. The audience just needed some livening up, some pander-monium. Once I had them listening, I transitioned into the good stuff, the polished bits that I used at Comedy Works. I knew to err on the side of clean so I kept it mostly PG, PG-13. They loved it. I had learned to read an audience by now and I was giving them what they wanted. I grew more confidant. I was goofy and loose. At the cash register there was an *order-up* bell next to the tip jar. I grabbed it in the middle of my set and began dinging it loudly after each punch line. I was in command. At the end of my set, I got a standing ovation. Thirty suburbanites moved to their feet. A couple of the bigger swinging dicks tipped me crisp twenties.

Lydia couldn't believe it. She sat with me on the outdoor patio after the show and we sipped free coffee and broke down my performance. She was like an anthropologist, she wanted to know everything: which parts were planned, what was off the top of my head, what material was newer, what was older. She asked me how I had come up with certain bits, offered up tags that I had not thought of. In that exact moment I watched Lydia pivot from indie rock to stand-up; I witnessed her metamorphosis into an alt-comedy fangirl right on that patio. She knew about Los Comicos and everything that I was doing, but I don't think she had fully put together that it was actually good, that my friends and I were performing some fine dick jokes up there in Denver, creating art equally of note—if not more—than the music she was consuming on a nightly basis. That night, I showed her. And she wanted in. Just like the newspaper had predicted. Comedy became her new punk rock.

She asked me if she moved back to Denver, could she maybe help out with shows. Work the door, sell drinks, run tech, whatever.

I often wonder what life would be like if I had said no.

THE GRAWLIX

"You're saying 'literally' too much," Lydia pointed out.

"No I'm not," I protested.

"You are. I counted. You said it four times last night. Four. In a ten-minute set. That's way too much."

"Did I really say it four times?"

"*Literally*. You say it a lot in general."

"I think you're right."

She was right. Her comedy instincts were dead-on. Lydia made everything I wrote better. Never huge overhauls, but a small suggestion here, a tweak there; she helped me get right to the essence of the joke and avoid all the fluff. She became a second set of eyes and ears. A secret writing partner. These were the type of intimate conversations a comic should allow only with another comic. But this was Lydia, my whip-smart little sister, my earliest collaborator. I let her in.

"What did you think of the e-mail exchange bit," I asked, "with the American Museum of Natural History in New York?"

"So fucking good. That crushed."

"It did do pretty well."

"But it needs one more back-and-forth. It was killing. The crowd wasn't ready for it to be over yet. One more short exchange between you and the museum, and the audience will lose their minds."

"But there isn't one more exchange. That was an actual back-and-forth. That's where the e-mails ended."

"So? No one in the audience knows that. Just make one up."

We were getting along famously, connecting in ways we hadn't since we were children. Our newfound proximity and a shared loved of comedy brought us closer together than ever before. Lydia worked the door at my shows. She sat in the booth and figured out lighting cues, played the videos. She lent a hand at the bar, she helped make flyers. And I needed her help. There was plenty of work to be done.

We had reemerged on the Denver comedy scene as a trio: Ben Roy, Andrew Orvedahl, and myself. It immediately felt right; Andrew and Ben were the two most talented comics I had ever met. We christened ourselves the Grawlix. "Grawlix" is the word one uses to refer to an omitted swear word in a comic strip, like this: *$!#@! The name was perfect, obscure, and pretentious, just like us.

We wanted to grow our audience, to attract the attention of the comedy world at large, so we decided to make a web series. Through the Denver comedy scene, we had gotten to know the Nix Brothers, Evan and Adam, two hive-minded brothers who were so in tune creatively everyone thought they were twins. They agreed to work with us, and thus was born the Grawlix web series *Behind the Scenes of ~~Denver's~~ the World's Best Comedy Show.*

We screened the first episodes at our live show, and the response was overwhelming—it was an immediate hit. Everyone seemed to respond to our on-screen dipshit trio, and we settled nicely into our roles as the smart-ass (moi), the lovable moron (Andrew), and the emotionally unstable maniac (Ben). We began uploading the episodes to Funny or Die, and in no time a Hollywood producer reached out to us about developing a script. We consulted with our reps, who informed us we didn't need some producer, we just needed to write a script ourselves and they could help us sell it.

So we did. I had been tinkering with a script that drew on my experiences as a substitute teacher in Denver public schools called *Those Who Can't.* I liked the high school setting but something was missing. I suggested we transfer our Grawlix characters into academia, and suddenly the ideas couldn't come to us fast enough. Andrew would be the moron gym teacher, blissfully unaware of his lack of athletic prowess. Ben would be a history teacher with a Howard Zinn bent—truth is the real punk rock. I would be the pretentious Spanish teacher, a guy who so desperately wants to be cool and who teaches the Queen's Castilian Spanish to primarily Mexican-American students. A world was born. Our reps loved it. More to the point, they told us they could sell it.

In the meantime, we just kept doing our Denver thing,

playing to sold-out audiences every month. We were becoming C-list local celebrities, like newscasters and used-car barons, except with actual personalities.

I had always wanted to make it in comedy from my hometown of Denver, but deep down I knew that was naïve. Now for the first time I started to actually believe that maybe I could do it. And I wanted nothing more. Why did I have to live somewhere I didn't want to live? Just to fit in to what was viewed as the comedy norm? I was proud of Denver, the little city that could. I was spending my twenties being involved in the arts scene in my hometown, pouring every ounce of myself into being someone from there, of there, like Neal Cassady but with dick jokes. And now my friends who were artists and musicians and comics were really starting to come into their own, myself included. So why did I have to leave all of that to fit some sort of coastal bias of what success means? There are great music scenes all over the country, I reasoned, why couldn't that be true of comedy? Bands come from everywhere. Why can't comics?

I was where I wanted to be.

And I loved having Lydia home. We ate lunch together three, four times a week. And I talked to her every single day on the phone. There was no one else in the world that was true with. Not Katie, the lovely girl I was beginning to date. Not my parents. Only Lydia. Not a day went by that I didn't talk to her. If that's not the definition of a best friend, I don't know what is.

My entire family was enjoying having her home.

My mother had leapt boldly into the dog show world, an insane *Best in Show* vortex that was the source of constant amusement. Lydia would often accompany her to competitions in small, forgotten cities along the Front Range. The agility dogs were their favorite. They would sit in the stands and watch the little guys tear ass around the course and laugh and laugh. Lydia began working at my dad's and Anna's law office, helping out with whatever was needed. Anna and my dad were considering passing on a case about a young black college student getting the shit beat out of him in a routine traffic stop. At first look there didn't seem to be enough evidence. Lydia did the intake and couldn't believe they hadn't taken it on. She pressed them until they acquiesced. It became the largest individual settlement in the history of Denver up until that point. Their client has become an anti-police-brutality activist in his own right. He tours around the country talking about what he went through to this day. Lydia was making her mark at the firm. She also ushered my dad through a tech revolution, updating his entire operating system to Macs, and teaching him Instant Messenger on his office network. I found their first effort folded in a drawer in Lydia's desk.

caytonholland (Lydia): hello
jholland (my dad): Hi
jholland: what up with that
jholland: can you have two or three people on same
     time, dad

caytonholland: what?

jholland: Can anna also talk with us at the same time, three at a time? How do you do that?

caytonholland: yes but she's not here right now

jholland: she's not that far away, repeat, how do that

caytonholland: I'm not telling; this is a dangerous tool in the wrong hands. Someone named Lucinda called about the Smith case. Do you know who that is?

jholland: I am waiting your last reply, you are falling behind, that is cruel, are you warm?

caytonholland: am I warm?

jholland: repeat, you warm?

caytonholland: yes, I'm warm. Who's Lucinda?

jholland: hi Lydia!

caytonholland: hi

jholland: hi

caytonholland: please answer my question about Lucinda

jholland: what do you want?

caytonholland: grrrr

jholland: hi Anna!

caytonholland: I'm Lydia.

jholland: your chat room name is wrong

caytonholland: forget it, I'll talk to you later

jholland: I miss you, why later?

jholland: hi Lydia!

jholland: hi!

My dad was boldly leaping into the twenty-first century, his daughters by his side. One as a partner, one a paralegal. Ostensibly. It was temporary. Some income while Lydia got her bearings in Denver.

We had family dinners together often, in the backyard of the house we grew up in. Anna would bring her fiancé Sam, my dad would barbecue, and we would sit and talk and drink wine and soak up the last moments of daylight. Those dinners felt like one of those good dramedies that comes along every few years, the one the networks so desperately hope take hold. They always revolve around a family unit coming to terms with adulthood, the delicate shift of children relating to their parents as grown-ups, relating to their siblings as peers. Done well those shows really sing.

And when those types of shows really swing for the fences, when the voice-over hammers home the lesson of the episode, and the family breaks bread as every character seizes their medium close-up of them laughing, of them as happy as they can allow themselves to be, you find yourself overcome. You choke on the emotion; your eyes wet with tears. Because you want that so bad for your family. You want that exact scene, that solid core, stronger than ever before, happy, unburdened, together. The children get married, the clan grows bigger, but it always comes back to the group gathered around that table. It always comes back to the family.

And we had that. For a brief moment, once Lydia returned to us, we had that. My mom, my dad, Anna, Lydia, me. We were all right where we were supposed to be, living our best lives, thriving. It may have been the happiest we ever were.

But looking back now it's impossible not to see that the cracks were beginning to form. Or maybe they were there all along, right beneath the surface, and we just didn't know to look for them—like little gnomes hidden in the paintings on the walls.

LITOST

"Lydia had a bit of a breakdown," my mother began. Her voice sounded thin, with sputtering stops and starts. You could tell she was trying not to cry, that she had been crying.

"Breakdown?" I said. "What kind of breakdown?"

I was in Mexico. I had met up with my buddy Gabe, who ran a student-travel company. He'd recently finished leading twenty high schoolers around the rural Mexican countryside. I'd recently had a *Denver Post* feature anoint me the next big thing to come out of Denver. We both had cause to celebrate. So why was my mom calling me? I didn't buy any temporary international plan. We had agreed to communicate via e-mail. Something was wrong. I knew it the second I saw the caller name pop up on my cell phone: *Home*.

That panicked feeling. It still happens to me all the time, whenever something seems off or irregular about the timing of a call. It happens more than you would think. My heart starts beating out of my chest; my breath becomes short.

This is it. The worst is here. Again. You knew the dark cloud would be coming back for you and the people you love. You knew you couldn't avoid it forever. Those times when it was gone, you were fooling yourself. You weren't safe. It always wins.

My mom filled me in. It was weird, she said. Lydia had come into my dad's office that morning and couldn't keep it together. She broke down in tears and started confessing all these things, like she couldn't keep them inside of her anymore, and was ashamed of them. She was like a pot boiling over, onto the stove, the floor. Everywhere. Lydia hadn't been able to sleep for months. She said she couldn't turn her brain off. That it howled at her. My mom said she kept talking like that. About her brain. As if it was someone else, someone controlling her, not a partner working in unison. *My brain won't let me.* Unable to sleep, Lydia would try to pass the time by reading but her brain *wouldn't allow her to.* She would read the individual letters in one word and then immediately scan back across them in reverse, reciting them in her mind, over and over, forwards, backwards, forwards, backwards, barely able to move on to the next word, let alone finish a sentence. An hour would pass and she wouldn't have read a paragraph. She felt like a prisoner in her own head.

My mom explained how my father had assured Lydia that it was okay. That she didn't need to feel any shame about telling us and that he wished she shared this sooner. He consoled her and told her that everything was going to be all right. We would get her some help, find a good therapist, do everything we possibly could to get to the bottom of it. My mom said Lydia seemed relieved to no longer be carrying the burden of her secret. I asked if I could call Lydia. My mom said she was asleep, sleeping like the dead.

I texted Lydia that I loved her and to call me when she woke up. I cracked a beer and headed out to the patio, overlooking the Pacific. I couldn't believe that I didn't know any of this. Why hadn't Lydia told me? Why hadn't I noticed? If she was so miserable and sleep-deprived, you would think that some of it would have spilled out into her everyday life. But she kept it so hidden.

Magical realism was her favorite genre of literature. Salman Rushdie, Gabriel García Márquez. She loved Milan Kundera. Anna turned her on to him. In *The Book of Laughter and Forgiving* Kundera writes, "*Litost* is a state of torment created by the sudden sight of one's own misery." Lydia had recently changed her screen name to it. Litost. Was that a cry for help? If so we missed it. I just thought it was a great screen name. Lydia's nickname was Lee. On certain platforms she went as "LeeToast." Nickname combined with obscure literary reference? Bravo, Little Sis! The internet awaits you.

But now, in the darkness of this "breakdown," it seemed sinister. It felt true.

"Is there a history of mental illness in your family?" Gabe asked me after I told him what was going on.

And suddenly I remembered, as if realizing for the first time, that there was. One I had felt so connected to when I was depressed in college, but had not thought about for years. But that didn't mean it wasn't still there.

My grandma's cousin Wallace threw himself off a bridge in Richmond, Virginia, in the forties. Had enough one day and leapt to his death off the Lee Bridge, right into the rushing James River down below. *Lee. Just like Lydia.* That was the story of Wallace; that was all anyone said about him. They didn't talk about his wife and children that he left behind. They didn't speculate about what drove him to it. Whenever anyone asked about it some relative would respond about not knowing anything about that whole mess. A suicide footnote. There was many an ancestor on my mom's side that spent time inside the walls of Virginia's Eastern State Mental Hospital, including one unfortunate relative named Emmett who was habitually in and out for "nerves." Their mental illness was nothing out of the ordinary, but it was also nothing to be spoken about.

Then there was my dad's sister Barbara, my aunt, whom we barely ever saw. She'd visit every few years and it was always, like, oh yeah. Dad has a sister. A manic sister. He let on very little about her as a child but the glimmer that we got was not pretty: her carrying on inappropriately with their cousin, her chasing after him with a knife when they were kids, her trying to poison him. My dad didn't talk about it much. Later I learned that Barbara ended up in a mental institute as a teenager and received shock therapy. Poor thing. But she was also brilliant. Several of her paintings hung in my parents' house. She had been a gifted piano player. *Just like Lydia.*

My dad left that family when he could; after his mother

passed away, he was off to go start his own new life. Barbara died years later in her fifties due to prescription drug complications: not an overdose, but issues from a body ravaged by medication. She didn't kill herself, my dad swears. At the time of her death, she had a boyfriend, her first in years. My dad remembers her as happy and in love. She hadn't taken her own life, but you got the sense that because of her mental illness, she never really got to live it either.

I remembered the last time I ever saw Barbara. She came for a visit and we walked a few blocks down Montview Boulevard to a nearby garage sale. She bought me a novelty mirror that I hung in the treehouse in the backyard. It would contort your face into all sorts of ghoulish fun-house masks when you looked in it. There were words painted on the glass in blue: *Objects in Mirror May be Closer Than They Appear.*

These people were all there in our bloodlines, victims of something sinister looming in our genes. Was Lydia becoming one of them?

"You okay man?" Gabe asked me.

I was crying.

"Come on," he said, patting me on the shoulder. "We should head out to a bar."

Lydia didn't reach out to me for the rest of that trip. I kept calling, e-mailing, doing everything I could to reach out to her. But I suppose she didn't feel up to it. I e-mailed my mom asking how she was. If there were any updates. She wrote back.

Things aren't going well for Lydia. She had a big meltdown today, crying and begging for medical help. Her doctor put her on a major anxiety drug—big, knockout dose—while he finds a shrink. She is sleeping now. Apparently she has been averaging only an hour or two a night for some time now. She has been very, very manic. We're all sad and scared. But we will keep a close eye on her and help her get what she needs. If she'll let us. Maybe it's good that she is finally getting to a place where she wants help. I love you. Be safe.

I asked my mom if I needed to cut my trip short to come home and help. She said to stay and enjoy myself. There was nothing I could do that they weren't already doing.

Gabe left Mexico a day before me and I spent a strange day in Sayulita alone. I moved to a crummy hotel off of the main zocalo. After a hot, mostly sleepless night, I awoke to find a boxing ring had been set up in the center of town. The streets were buzzing. There would be fights that morning.

A crew of young boys in gloves and headgear lounged on the ropes, waiting for their respective turns in the ring. But before they could fight, the organizer of the event got into the middle of the ring and whipped the crowd into a frenzy. He talked about how education was abhorrent in the area. There were no opportunities for the youth. Boxing, he continued, represented a viable way out. If these young boys trained hard and remained focused, the entire world was theirs for the taking. Who knew what they could achieve! And it all started right there, right then, in that boxing ring in Sayulita. For him it was that simple, that linear: boxing, hard work, escape, success. As if nothing else could get in the way. As if life didn't have so much else in store for every little fighter that day.

A spirited clanging of the bell, then the fights. First there were six-year-olds, then eight-year-olds, then ten, and so on by twos all the way into adulthood. Every twenty minutes another pairing of young boys took the ring and proceeded to beat the living shit out of each other, one boy in red trunks, one in blue. They fought like their lives depended on it, like there was only one carrot dangling there in front of them, like there wasn't enough to go around.

I didn't have the stomach for it. I couldn't even get off in some wannabe-Hemingway way, pat myself on the back for being in a foreign country alone and watching something violent, like real men are supposed to do. All I saw were two desperate little boys bludgeoning one another when they should be catching insects in jars and going to birthday parties. While the audience howled for more. I left the square and headed down to the beach, depressed, wondering why life has to be so goddamn hard for some people.

STILL LIFE OF LYDIA

The next few months played out like a ball of knots, impossible to unwind. None of it made sense.

"Maybe you'd be happier somewhere else," I said to Lydia. "Somewhere away from us. Back in Colorado Springs. Or you could go back to Ecuador if it would help you feel better."

I didn't sugarcoat anything. This was Lydia. We could be straight-up with each other. No bullshit. I felt like my shadow was eclipsing her, Anna's too. Did she need to get away from us? Did she need to be alone somewhere?

"That's fucking ridiculous," Lydia said. "I'm not threatened by you guys. I love you guys. And I'm happy being home. This is where I want to be. I'm just going through some shit right now."

She was already seeing a new shrink—her second since her confession to my father—and she was taking prescriptions pills to help her sleep regularly. It was a strange turn of events, she insisted, but one that was isolated.

"I already feel more in control of my brain," she said.

So we believed her. Why wouldn't we? We had no reason not to.

And sometimes she seemed like she was doing so well.

Like one night, I got home from a weekend of shows out of town. It was late on a Sunday evening, and I was exhausted. I just wanted to hang out with my dog, eat some sugar cereal, catch up on my DVR. Lydia had other plans. She called me and reported that she was having an impromptu backyard party and that my attendance was required. It was all very matter of fact.

"Not a chance, Lee," I said. "I'm spent."

She was undeterred. Lydia never accepted a first offer. She let loose with her pitch: tons of comics were going to be there, all my friends. She was shy and didn't want to host a party without me. Everyone was wanting her to do better, to not retreat inward, this was her way of doing just that.

It was Lydia to a T: impassioned defense of an irrational position. In Lydia's mind a dinner party at six on a Saturday was no different than a throw-down on a Sunday at midnight. Weren't they both just gatherings of people? So she kept after me, relentlessly. I shot down every entreaty, she just reloaded and kept firing. This was our brother-sister ping-pong; a game we knew quite well. I knew that I would lose. Because Lydia always won. She was a mule-child, as stubborn as they come. After twenty minutes of back-and-forth I caved and told her I'd be right over.

It was a late-summer night. I walked the seven or eight

blocks to her house. I skipped the front door and hopped over the side gate which never opened right. It was like I landed in a painting: *Still Life of Lydia.* Tiki torches lined the thin portion of side-yard leading to the back. On the picnic table, dishes of fruit and cheese and crackers were artfully arranged. There was a cooler of beer on ice. There was music playing. Twenty of our friends were in attendance, all laughing and enjoying themselves. Lydia's dogs Anya and Wren were out, yapping and jumping and loving the company and attention. It was beautiful. Absolutely perfect. A snapshot of the kind of life that you would hope your sibling leads. And there was Lydia in the center of it all. She didn't notice me at first so I just watched her: the little hostess, so normal, so beautiful, so vibrant. When she saw me she lit up, relieved that I finally showed. Her eyes sparkled at me, as if to say, "See, Adam? Aren't you glad you came?!" And I was. I really was.

How could she possibly be doing so poorly when here she was, thriving?

Because Lydia had become a pendulum, capable of opposing extremes. For every yin, there was a yang.

Like another night, we had a Grawlix live show and Lydia was flaking, again. She had started doing that a lot. I kept calling her but she wouldn't answer her phone. The other comics were backstage, grumbling. We were waiting to do a tech rehearsal but it was impossible without the person running tech. And the show started in an hour. Finally, Lydia answered and let loose with a string of vague apologies and explanations for her behavior. She didn't have gas in her car. Her computer was messed up. Also she was feeling socially awkward. I called bullshit on every excuse. She just reloaded and kept firing. Brother-sister ping-pong. Of course I was bound to lose.

I told her to just get to the goddamn show already. She said she would send her boyfriend Zack instead. He'd be there in a half hour. He was there forty-five minutes later, carrying a laptop with a zip drive Lydia gave him full of all our tech cues, the video for the show, the music. He was apologetic and eager to help, like somehow this was his fault and not my little sister's fuck-up. I met him on the street and ushered him past a line of people waiting angrily in the rain. Doors were supposed to be open fifteen minutes ago.

That same girl I marveled at in her backyard, I was now furious with. I had no patience for any of it. I was totally uncharitable in those moments. I sent Lydia bitchy texts like *Thanks a fucking lot, Lee.* I tried to have empathy after her breakdown but the days grew into weeks and then months and Lydia's behavior kept flip-flopping so often it was impossible to live in that headspace of understanding. Sometimes she was great and completely on top of things, other times she was a total flake. It infuriated me.

I couldn't contextualize. I'd had twenty-six years of Lydia as normal, capable, reliable, and that was all I'd had. I was not used to this new version. And I resented it. I helped her, consoled her, asked her how it was going with her third, fourth, and fifth new shrinks and where her head was at. But I also grew frustrated. Often. Like come on, Lee. Get your shit together.

Anna understood. We commiserated. Bitched about Lydia fucking up. She blew tech at a big trial for Anna and my dad. They needed her to compile hundreds of pieces of evidence and show the slides to the jury. Instead she came into the courtroom so exhausted she was barely functional. She moped at the prosecution table like a petulant teen. Anna had to take over and execute the grunt paralegal work in addition to trying the case. Seven months pregnant. With a three-year-old at home. Anna was so exhausted and hormonal she cried in the courthouse bathroom during recesses. She was just so over it all. Lydia had completely dropped the ball.

The memories continued to stack up, one on top of the other. A sloppy pile.

Lydia started dating a new guy, some DJ over a decade older than her. I ran into him at Whole Foods once. He approached me right there in the middle of the fruits and vegetables and told me he had nothing but good intentions with Lydia. We were casual acquaintances, had a few friends in common. Then he started hooking up with my little sister. I wanted to tell him to fuck off. That she was a child compared to him. But I just shook his hand.

Lydia's ex, Zach, moved across the alley. They remained close friends. He was intimately familiar with her mental state and checked on her often. Including the day after

Thanksgiving, when he found her strung out on too much Ambien. He took her to the ER. She made him swear he wouldn't tell any of us, but Zach felt like he couldn't keep it a secret. So he cheated and called Sam, Anna's husband. Not a blood-relation anyway. Sam immediately told Anna. They were in Lincoln, Nebraska, at the time for Thanksgiving with Sam's family. So Anna called my parents. They hurried to the hospital. I had a Grawlix show that night. Last Friday of the month. Lydia was supposed to work it. By that point I was so accustomed to her not showing I always had a backup on hand. I didn't even learn she was in the hospital until after the show. As far as I knew she just wasn't returning my texts. Flaking again.

They didn't pump her stomach because the pills had already dissolved inside her. They just monitored her levels. They talked about a psych hold but Lydia insisted it wasn't an overdose, it was a mistake. My mother and father helped convince the doctors that was the case. They still believed Lydia. Or at least wanted to. If alarm bells were going off, no one was acknowledging them. Not yet. It seemed feasible. Lydia was so tiny, barely a hundred pounds, of course the pills would hit her like a Mack truck. She just needed to be more careful. What was she thinking?

My mom took her back to her house that night and stayed with her. All Lydia cared about, my mom told us, was getting in touch with her new boyfriend. She wanted him to come retrieve her from the hospital. She wanted him to come over to her house after she got out. She seemed to want to use this scare as some sort of fucked-up leverage. Their relationship was fraught with manipulation on both sides. None of us liked it, or him. He was having a bad effect on her. Christ, she ended up in the fucking hospital.

Memories.

How could this be happening? To *us*? The Magnificent Cayton-Hollands? These were not the story lines we were supposed to be pursuing. This was not the road we were supposed to be heading down.

Was this our tornado? Our disaster? Our *very special episode*? If so, I didn't want it anymore. Lydia might, but I didn't. Our dad was right. To hope for such things was ridiculous. I longed for the bland normalcy of our everyday. I wanted Lydia working the Grawlix, not in the hospital. I wanted the family unit in all their glorious predictability. I wanted to be back in Kansas, instead of here, in this fucked-up Oz.

Click your heels together three times.

There's no place like home. There's no place like home. There's no place like home.

But it didn't work.

And then things really started getting bad.

CURSED

That was the summer that the clouds descended. Life became distorted; familiar but strange. Every week something new, and terrible. Those things that you only hear about happening to other people were beginning to happen to us.

Call it magical realism.

Is started when the Denver Police Department raided my house. I had just come home for the day and took my dog Annabel for a walk. Mere moments after my return there was a furious pounding on the front door.

"DPD open up!" the voice on the other side bellowed.

I squinted through the peephole. A fat pink fingertip was blocking my view.

"Yeah right," I said, figuring one of my friends was pretty proud of themselves at that moment.

"DENVER POLICE! OPEN THE FUCKING DOOR!"

This was no joke.

I stole a few moments to put away the by-now-hysterical Annabel and opened the door. Four uniformed officers burst into my house. They forced my hands behind my back and slammed my face down on the entry table.

"Are we gonna need handcuffs?" they said.

No. We were not.

"Do you have a warrant?" I asked, the lawyer's son.

Two detectives promptly glided through the doorway, chests puffed like peacocks, badges bobbing on the chains around their necks.

"Here's your warrant," the lead detective said, handing me a piece of paper. "Have you been downloading some stuff illegally, sir?"

The question took me off guard. Downloading stuff? What kind of stuff? I stammered something about *Friday Night Lights*, the last season of *Six Feet Under*, but other than that I had no idea what he was talking about. Well, we'll see about that, he informed me. And so for the next hour and a half I sat in my living room detained while the detectives combed through my laptop upstairs. The uniformed officers stood within arms length, making sure I didn't try to escape. They peppered me with questions but I remained silent.

"Can I call my dad?" my only words.

They wouldn't allow it so I didn't say a thing, remembering my father's advice growing up: *You don't talk to police. You talk to lawyers.*

Slowly, whatever the fuck was going on came out. Did I have a password on my wireless router? No. I did not. I tried to put one on there but I'm pretty much computer-illiterate and it was harder than one click so I figured there was no harm in letting the bike messengers and vegan farmers next door enjoy the fruits of my free internet.

Well, someone was downloading some pretty awful stuff, I was informed, and all signs pointed to the router in my bedroom closet.

Awful stuff? What kind of awful stuff?

That kind of awful stuff. Jared from Subway awful stuff.

After combing through every download made on my MacBook Pro for the past who-knows-how-long, the DPD learned exactly what kind of stuff I'm into, and that it is decidedly not that.

"Ninety-nine percent of the time this is what happens," the lead detective said. "We trace the signal to someone's house who had no idea this was going on. They don't have a password-protected network and, surprise, someone's downloading horrendous shit."

He spoke to me like I was a fucking idiot. Like of course this was the logical outcome of not having a password-protected wireless signal. There was no remorse in his voice. No "Sorry to traumatize you and your dog in the privacy of your household at five on a Tuesday afternoon."

"Well is it the neighbors?" I asked him.

Probably not, he told me. They'd check everybody out, due diligence and all that, but most of the time it was some pervert driving around in a van looking for free wireless signals like mine. They'd stay on the case. They'd catch the guy.

And then he was gone. As was the other detective, and the uniformed officers. I locked my door after them and that was that for my run-in with the Denver Police Department Internet Crimes Division. Except for the fact that I couldn't stop shaking for the next two days. Or the fact that I couldn't fall asleep that night, or how the next morning Annabel lost her mind when the paper landed on the front doorstep, an occasion that never even roused either of us from our slumber prior to the raid. Or the fact that the whole block watched the police pull two cars onto my front lawn and burst through the door.

I threw away my old router, got a new laptop, a new password, but I was shaken. I talked to Anna and my dad about legal action but there was really nothing to be done. The experience stayed with me. Every time I saw a cop it would come back up. Walking through the airport en route to a gig I'd see two police officers walking down the concourse and I would shudder with fear as I pictured them slamming me up against a wall, arresting me for any number of thought crimes. I started hating cops, every one I saw. It wasn't hard. Children of civil rights attorneys are hardwired that way.

Then a cop got shot in the head in broad daylight in City Park and my empathy was reawakened. It was at Jazz in the Park, a favorite Denver summer Sunday pastime. Some cheesy band plays at the boathouse grandstand by the lake, food trucks descend, and the young professionals lie on blankets and drink wine. Sometimes the mayor's wife steps up to the mic and belts out a few songs. It's lovely. And quaint. Old couples holding hands, young parents with children and lawn chairs and coolers and baseball gloves in the park that I grew up in, the park that I called home. It's old Denver. But on this night there was an argument between some gang members on the perimeter of the event. And a police officer stepped into the fray to keep the peace. And a gun was produced. And like that she was gone. She was a mother of two, the paper said. Thirty-two years old. My age at the time. Lydia was at Jazz in the Park that night too. She heard the shots.

The heat was unrelenting that summer, an atypical spell with temperatures in the one hundreds for weeks in a row. And no rain whatsoever. Any Coloradoan knows what that means. Sure enough, late June, a few weeks after the officer died, the first forest fire ignited in the hills beyond Fort Collins, the college town about an hour and a half north of Denver. Wildfires are nothing new in Colorado but they're always in obscure places, some unfortunate patch of mostly desolate Rocky Mountain terrain. Fort Collins was familiar. Colorado State University is in Fort Collins. New Belgium Brewery is in Fort Collins. I've dated girls from Fort Collins. And while the High Park Fire up north was horrible, it turned out to be nothing compared to the Waldo Canyon Fire that devoured parts of Colorado Springs to the south a few days later. It was coming at us from both sides. Ash and smoked filled the air.

That's the fire you saw on the news. The area that Obama

visited. The most destructive fire in Colorado history. It was like a war zone. Thirty-two thousand people evacuated, hundreds of homes destroyed. On the worst night of the conflagration I had a show and a few of the people in the audience were from Colorado Springs, where Lydia went to college and lived for those few years afterward. They had fled to Denver because every hotel room in the Springs was booked. After the show they showed us pictures on their cell phones of the apocalyptic scenes back home—giant, shrieking flames threatening to devour a highway crammed full of cars crammed full of earthly possessions: photo albums, clothing racks, dogs and cats. It was end-of-days shit, and between the fire to the north and the fire to the south, there was a feeling of impending doom in Denver. Like we were next up. The Front Range of Colorado is a place where it's easy to get your bearings. The mountains are always to the west, a simple frontier truism. But the smoke was so thick during those wildfires you couldn't see the mountains. You looked to the west and it was just a hazy wall of angry sky. It was impossible not to feel lost and scared, like something truly terrible was bearing down on us.

We checked Lydia into the psych ward not long after the fire was contained. There was no fooling us this time. Not again. Do we get a pat on the back for that one? She'd bounced from shrink to shrink, keeping them all at arms length, bristling when one asked to talk to her parents. She was too smart for them. She outfoxed one after another until eventually she'd arranged a scenario where a psychiatrist would just prescribe different drugs for her to see how they worked, a bizarre and increasingly severe cocktail that sent her from high to low with no apparent regularity or regimen: Adderall, Ativan, Lorazepam.

She'd quit working for my dad. It was too stressful, she said. She'd begun working at a hipster Mexican restaurant a few blocks from my house. She was their star employee; they wanted her to take all the shifts she could handle. But she only worked a few days a week. Said she needed those other days to relax and focus on her mental well-being. Which meant taking a bunch of antipsychotic meds to knock herself out for the entire day. We didn't know any of this until she showed up to a dinner barely able to stand. She kept it hidden after that first scare, that first trip to the ER.

We met at a Vietnamese restaurant on Federal and Lydia sat down at the table and slumped over in her chair. She told us that she had taken sleeping pills earlier and forgotten about the dinner and she apologized. She just wanted to sleep away all the hours when she wasn't working. Our eyes darted around the table at each other. This was clearly a problem. She went out to sleep in my dad's car while we ate. I went to check on her in the middle of our meal. My dad had moved his car around to the back of the restaurant because it just seemed safer there. I peeked my head in the window and watched her little chest rise and fall in the backseat. I watched my sister breathe. A chef on the back staircase smoking a cigarette smiled at me.

"She very tired," he said to me, cheerfully, in broken English. Then he drew a finger to his eyeball. "I keep an eye on her."

That was our Father's Day, 2012.

Her friend called me the next morning to let me know that Lydia had bailed on going to their mutual friend's wedding. She said she just wanted to sleep. I went over to check on her and I could barely rouse her. I grabbed her by the shoulders and shook her, which elicited moments of coherence, mumbled words. *Sleep. Pills. Didn't take too many.* I called my parents and Anna and the entire nuclear family assembled around her bed. She was nauseous. We took her to the bathroom to try to get her to throw up and she collapsed on the cold, black-and-white tile floor—just like I had my freshmen year in college, at my worst. It was then that she confessed that she had looked up online just how many of her antipsychotic meds she could take without killing herself, but to completely knock her out. And she had taken exactly that many. It was not a suicide attempt, she insisted. It was an attempt not to exist day after day. Which was just as bad. I picked her up in my arms and carried her to my car. Anna and I sped to Denver Health a few blocks away. Anna got out and tracked down a wheelchair. We threw Lydia into it and pushed her through the doors of the ER. They had no doubts about her condition. She sped past everyone, all the people in the waiting room mired in their own personal tragedies. We just blew by them. We watched as they hooked Lydia up to a cavalcade of beeping machinery and flushed her system with fluids. She became conscious and seemed to resent everything. She wouldn't talk to us. Wanted to use our phones to text her boyfriend. We were having none of it.

What the fuck is happening, Lydia?

A mandatory seventy-two-hour hold for a psych evaluation wasn't even a question. And so once a bed was available they moved Lydia up to the fifth floor to the psych ward, east side of the building. Nonviolent. It was surprisingly decent. For some reason I was expecting a nightmare. Howling lunatics screaming Bible passages, shit smeared on the walls. But everything was clean and sterile, quiet and calm.

They let us visit as much as we wanted. We'd bring her books and meals and keep her company. We'd sit at the communal table while Denver's destitute crazies shuffled past us in various states of decrepitude, and we'd chuckle to one another at the bizarre things they would say. While Anna and I ate lunch with her one day, we were stunned to find that a man we knew named Danny was there on the same ward with Lydia. We had not seen him in years. When we were children Danny appeared out of the blue one day, just rang the doorbell at my parents' house with some sob story about needing money. My parents helped him out and he became a regular visitor after that. He'd show up every few months, always with a pitiful new tale. Occasionally he'd bring us gifts—a basketball for me, a TV that he wanted to give to the family. My parents would refuse the offerings and give him a few dollars and send him on his way. He was clearly mentally ill then, but essentially harmless. Sometimes he would come when my parents were away, and we were instructed not to open the door on those occasions. Harmless, but still. When no one answered he would ring the doorbell over and over, he'd shout loud hellos and we'd go completely still, like frightened animals.

It's Danny! Stay quiet!

He'd peer through the windows to see if anyone was home and we would scramble to stay out of eyeshot and hide behind furniture. We'd look at each other in those moments and giggle nervously, frightened children in a high-stakes game of hide-and-go-seek. Then Danny just stopped coming by. We'd see him around town sometimes. Denver's still a small enough place that that type of stuff happens. But then we stopped seeing him altogether. If we thought about him at all, I'm sure we figured he was dead. And here he was on the psych ward, some twenty years later, worse for the wear, sure, but Danny nonetheless. Danny!

Two rooms down from Lydia.

It made us laugh, the insanity of it all, we Cayton-Holland three baffled and tickled at how we were suddenly seeming to exist in the sad works of art on which we fixated. But those moments gave way to teary panic when we removed the rose-colored, indie-film lenses from our eyes. This was just our little sister. Struggling. In a psych ward.

It was devastating. We begged her to level with us. Was she suicidal? Did she want to kill herself? Because we could keep her there. Or send her somewhere nicer, somewhere she could get the help she needed, long-term, some asylum in Switzerland, whatever it took.

"We're not going to let you leave us," we told her. "There's three of us, not two. Three. You get it? You understand?"

She started bawling. She said she did. She wanted to get better. She was going to get better. This was the wake-up call she needed.

They ushered us into an antiseptic white room for Lydia's exit interview, a safe place for families to wring their hands before welcoming their wounded member back into the outside world. The doctors wanted to speak to us alone before Lydia joined. I wondered what they thought of us, whether they blamed us. Were we the root cause of all the problems the little girl they had been examining for the past seventy-two hours was experiencing? The mother, the father, the sister, the brother—the four-headed shadow consuming Lydia.

We told them how much we loved Lydia, how she was the smartest person any of us knew. They agreed. They said Lydia was one of the smartest patients they had ever encountered. Which is why the help that she needed had to be dictated by her. We could push her all we wanted but she had to be in charge of helping herself.

In charge of helping herself? What good would that do?

She had been in charge of helping herself for the past year, hop-scotching from shrink to shrink, and all we had to show for it was two overdoses and a little sister who just wanted to sleep her life away.

Still, I knew what they meant. Stubborn was not a strong enough word to describe Lydia. She was bullheaded, impossible. If she didn't want to do something, there was absolutely no getting her to come around.

When we were kids our neighbors had a trampoline that they used to let us jump on all the time. Their children were grown and out of the house, so they didn't mind having some young kids in their backyard playing every now and then. But it was a delicate balance. You had to space out your requests, not overstay your welcome. We didn't want to tax their goodwill. Lydia could care less. Whenever Anna and I determined it was time to go home, she would simply refuse. There was no reasoning with her, no explaining the diplomacy of the situation. She just wanted to jump forever. Anna and I would insist but Lydia wouldn't have it. She would lie facedown in the center of the trampoline in an attempt to make herself as heavy as possible so that we couldn't remove her. Eventually, Anna would take her legs, I'd grab her arms and we'd struggle to carry her home while she remained completely limp in nonviolent resistance. It was highly effective. So I was relieved when she came into the room that day and seemed compliant. The look on her face was pure heartbreak. She didn't want to do this to us anymore, she said, to her family, the people she lived and breathed for, the beneficiaries of her self-taught agnostic prayers. She was not going to hurt herself anymore. She was going to get better. For her. For us. She promised. This was the bottom. There would be no lower rung.

I was encouraged when I came back to the hospital later that day to pick her up. She signed a few pieces of paper and they returned to her a Ziploc freezer bag full of prescriptions that we had taken from her medicine cabinet, a desperate attempt to arm the doctors with as much information as possible when we rushed her to the ER. I took the bag from the clerk before Lydia could.

"We should probably throw these away, right Lee?"

She agreed. We tossed them in a trash can in the hallway of the hospital. Her lip was quivering. I hugged her.

"This happens, Lydia," I said. "You're gonna get better."

"I know," she said. "I will."

I believed it. I wonder if Lydia did too. Or was she so talented an actress she could just lie in such a moment? Right to my stupid, tear-streaked face.

We walked home through the neighborhood and I saw her back into her house. We hung out for a few hours, watched a movie, and when I left I made her promise not to do anything rash, to call us if she needed anything, or if she was feeling upset or depressed. Then I said goodbye. It was a long, scary night but she was there the next morning, and the one after that. Then the next few. She started playing the piano again. She started doing more yoga. Started look-ing for new shrinks, got off the meds. She seemed down but not out. She was trying to get back to being herself. She was funny and caustic. A number of guys had reached out to her to hang out in the wake of her hospital stint. I don't know if one was related to the other but I encouraged her to go out with them. I wanted to steer her away from that other relationship, which seemed increasingly manipula-tive and fucked up. I teased her about all the attention she was receiving. She pondered the situation for a moment.

"Yeah," she concluded. "I think I'm just strange-enough-looking that pseudointellectuals are proud of themselves for finding someone like me attractive."

Her wit was intact. She was still depressed and morbid, but seemingly less so. I texted her every night.

You okay?
Yeah. Just sad.
Sad normal, or sad bad?
Sad normal. Just want to sleep.
Sleep normal? Like with no pills?
Sleep normal. No pills.
K. You nice. ☺
You nicer. ☺

She was doing the best she knew how, trying to focus on things that made her happy. Our cousin Griffin came to visit and she made us all go see *The Avengers*, Joss Whedon her most current obsession *célèbre*. As we drove out to a mammoth movie theater in the suburbs, Lydia fangirled the entire way. She had already seen the movie twice and wanted to make sure we knew exactly what we should be looking for as we watched for the first time. She was so quintessentially herself. So geeky and obsessive and normal. *There she is,* I thought. *There's my little sister.* For the first time in a long while I thought she was going to beat this thing.

Meanwhile the cosmos kept throwing curveballs.

"What the fuck is wrong with Colorado?" read the text on my phone when I awoke.

It was from an old friend, a college buddy. Others began pouring in.

You okay?
You alive?
Were you at the premiere?

I wasn't. But many others were. Gathered with excitement in a suburban movie theater just like the one where we watched *The Avengers* at mere days before. But this wasn't Marvel. This was DC. *The Dark Night Rises.* On that horrible night in Aurora. You know the story. Some nut job in a long string of Colorado nut jobs attacked the movie theater with guns and smoke bombs and high-caliber weaponry and all the other internet-acquired accoutrement of the modern, twenty-first-century psychopath. It was like some Columbine acid flashback. And the death toll rose to sickening amounts, men, women, and children, all attended to by devastated and shell-shocked emergency services teams. The community was traumatized. It was shocking, and heartbreaking. Obama came out again. His second emergency trip to Colorado that summer.

The darkness seemed relentless.

What was happening? Why could we not pull out of this nosedive? The police raiding my house, the murder in the park, the fires, Lydia, now this? When was this going to end? Or at least relent? I needed a break from it all. I needed to not feel like everything was falling apart, like the ground beneath me was crumbling.

Then I got the news that I had been accepted into the Montreal Just for Laughs Festival as a New Face. And the clouds momentarily lifted.

NEW FACES

"In my hand right now I'm holding more filmmaking technology than Orson Welles had when he filmed *Citizen Kane*."

With that Patton Oswalt held up his cell phone for all of us gathered there in that Montreal Hyatt conference room to see: the young comics, the vets, the industry, and anyone else lucky enough to score a ticket to his State of Comedy keynote address.

"I'm holding the same amount of cinematography, postediting, sound editing, and broadcast capabilities as you have at your TV network," he said. "In a couple of years, it's going to be fucking equal. I see what's fucking coming. This isn't a threat; this is an offer. We like to create. We're the ones who love to make shit all the time. You're the ones who like to discover it and patronize it and support it and nurture it and broadcast it. Just get out of our way when we do it."

I felt as if he were speaking directly to me. And I needed to hear it. Right then. Right there.

My head was already swimming, as any newbie comic

at Just For Laughs would be. I had auditioned twice in the previous two years and not been accepted to Montreal. Third time was the charm. One great set in Hollywood had sealed the deal. Twenty "New Faces" from across North America had been selected to come to Montreal, and I was one of them. Congratulations, kid. Welcome to the big leagues. I was on my way to perform for the entire industry as someone anointed by the comedy gods on high, someone worth watching, perhaps even signing! Me! Adam Cayton-Holland! I was a funny, shiny, brand-spanking-new face!

Gather round ye Hollywood agents and managers and lawyers! There's fresh fish to be raped!

Upon landing in Montreal I checked my phone and learned that I had been named one of the Top Twenty-Five Comics to Watch by *Esquire*. A few hours later an article appeared in *Wired* in which I had done an interview about what it meant to be selected as a New Face. Arguably the two biggest pieces of press I'd ever gotten, in the course of a few hours of being in Canada! They were clickbait articles deliberately timed to harness the full hype of the festival, but the effect was immediate. Like that I was one of *the* buzz-worthy new comics. My phone blew up. Friends from all over congratulating me. My manager telling me so-and-so wanted to grab lunch or coffee while we were here in Montreal. I hadn't even performed yet.

Lydia texted me every half hour for updates. I called her often. She was the only one I could properly gush to without feeling gauche. She was the only person on the planet as absolutely thrilled as I was. She wanted to experience it vicariously. She was so proud of me. She wasn't broken or depressed in those exchanges, she was elated. All the conversations we had about comedy, all those day-after breakfasts tagging jokes, all those shows, it felt like it was beginning to pay off. Who knew what this was the start of? We practically squealed.

The room was packed for my first set at Place des Arts. Capacity. The festival gives each New Face comic three spots, but people really only come out for that first set. Montreal is a buyer's game: big agencies looking to sign young new talent. That first set becomes the snap judgment that all of the industry makes about you. No one comes to that second or third New Faces showcase. It's one and done. And I could feel the pressure. It felt like all of Hollywood was watching. But I was ready for it. And I crushed. It was arguably the set of the night. Everyone wanted a piece of me after that. My days quickly filled with meetings, a baptism by fire on the nature of schmoozy LA bullshittery. I soaked it up. Who doesn't like free meals and being told how great they are? And when I wasn't doing that I was being added to shows left and right, both by the festival and by friends I had met over the years performing in Denver and around the country.

Adam, you're up here?! Want to hop on my show?

I did. And when I wasn't performing comedy, I was watching my favorite comics perform. Then partying with them at the lobby bar until dawn. Like I was one of them. The Just for Laughs festival was all that the comedy prophets had foretold. It was head-swelling stuff. A comic and a comedy nerd's wet dream. My hotel bedside table was filling up with business cards of agents and managers and producers, all of whom asked about the script I had written with the Grawlix, *Those Who Can't*. They also kept asking when I was going to "make the move." I had heard the words "Los Angeles" so many times I was on the verge of typing it instinctually every time I visited a travel website. I had been all about Denver for so long, had climbed to what I figured was the top, it seemed like now was the time to make the leap. My family would understand. My city would understand. Career opportunity and all that. Big fish, little pond. Time to grow into a shark. I was thinking big. Comedy, television, movies, it all seemed possible, right at my fingertips, if only I made the move to sunny Los Angeles!

Sitting in that Montreal Hyatt conference hall listening to Patton Oswalt tell industry and comics alike that the system as they knew it was dead and gone, I made up my mind that I would not be moving. That speech gut-checked me in the best way possible. I was going to stay the course. I was going to keep making videos with my buddies in the Grawlix. I was going to keep contributing to a flourishing Denver comedy scene that was gaining a national reputation, and I was going to make it on my own terms. The way I wanted to make it. Surrounded by the Magnificent

Cayton-Hollands in the city that I loved. Fuck this Hollywood bullshit. That wasn't me. I was going to keep doing things the only way I knew how, outside the established system.

I flew back to Denver inspired and determined. I could see my future laid out in front of me. I had a plan.

How's that saying go again?

Want to make God laugh? Tell him your plans.

LOVE YOU ALL

My mom picked me up at the airport. I was exhausted from Montreal. I had been up all night partying. I'd gotten maybe three hours of sleep. We had breakfast at a diner on Tower Road and I caught her up. She wanted to know everything, all the gossip. I told her all about the festival and let her know that I didn't want to move to LA, not now, probably not ever. She seemed relieved. She didn't say anything to that effect, she would never put that pressure on me, but I could feel it; she liked having her kids around her. We made her laugh.

I asked her how Lydia was doing.

"You know," she said. "The same."

When I got home my friend Andrew from the Grawlix called. I figured he wanted to hear about Montreal, see if there had been any movement on our *Those Who Can't* script. I let it go to voicemail. I'd catch him up later. For now, I needed to nap. But I checked his message before I climbed into bed. His voice sounded agitated, embarrassed. Like he didn't want to have to tell me what he was about to tell me. Lydia had made a scene at the bar the night before, the shitty vegan restaurant where her boyfriend worked as a DJ and where a bunch of comics liked to hang out. There had been screaming and yelling and they had kicked her out of the place. Andrew apologized for having to be the bearer of this disturbing news but he figured I'd want to know.

I dialed Lydia up and called her out. She immediately became hysterical. I told her to come over so we could talk in person. She was there in minutes and she broke down on my living room floor, wailing about how she couldn't stand that I would get a voicemail like that, that people would perceive her as crazy. She found her own behavior pathetic. She said that she was disgusted with herself.

Litost.

I picked her up, dusted her off, took her for some waffles at her favorite new place, the only place she had eaten in weeks. Belgian waffles with Nutella. I tried to calm her down the best I could and then I drove her home. I couldn't do it anymore. Couldn't cheer her up or be responsible for her right in that moment. I was too tired. I called the family to report her most recent breakdown. I handed off the baton of monitoring to another Magnificent Cayton-Holland and went back home to go to sleep.

We were all so over it. It was constant vigilance and it was trying. That's the thing no one tells you about depression. How exhausting it is to those around the person suffering. How all-consuming it is, and how selfish. There's not a lot of "how are you doing" coming out of someone who is truly depressed. Their gloom is the focus. Their misery is all that gets discussed. And you get sick of it. There's only so much of someone else's despair you can take.

Sorry to hear it, Lee. You'll get through it. You always do, right?

The next day we received an e-mail from Lydia at 9:50 a.m.

"Love you all."

That's it. That was the entire message.

Anna called me immediately. Did I get that e-mail? I did. It was probably nothing, we agreed. A welcome, chipper departure from somewhere within her seemingly ceaseless depression. Still, I should go check on Lydia, we concluded. She wasn't answering her phone. My house was the closest. It made sense I would be the one to go.

I drove over and let myself in with the key Lydia had given me. The dogs were in the backyard. That was odd. Usually when she slept in they'd be up in the bedroom with her, whining to go out. Instead I could hear them barking in the backyard, but the house itself seemed still and silent. Something was wrong. I knew it immediately. And yet I just kept going. I couldn't stop.

I made my way up the staircase. The staircase is huge in my memory, steep and dark, with walls that loom. The Haunted Mansion. Finally, I reached the top. I stood there on the landing for a moment. I took a breath. Then I opened her bedroom door.

She was there, in the bed, perfectly still. A small gun in her hand. A trickle of blood down her blue lips. It wasn't messy, not what you would expect. It was almost serene. Calm. There lies Lydia, in her final resting place.

They say you go out of your body at the sight of such trauma. That it's too much for you to process in your actual skin and bones and so you depart from yourself at that moment and everything seems fake, not real.

That didn't happen to me. I felt everything. A battering ram slammed into my chest. I felt a force unlike anything I've ever experienced in my life. I screamed. I fell to the floor. I still shake when I think about it. It wasn't out-of-body. It was visceral, tangible. *That* I can remember, can still feel, can never forget.

Then immediately after, it all became false. Like a switch was flipped. Like it wasn't even her anymore. Or me. That's when I went out of my body. I drifted above myself and watched, as though I were witnessing a scene from a play or a movie. *Harold and Maude*. A hoax.

This blood is just makeup! This has to be makeup. This gun in her hand—this fucking gun in her hand?! This is a prop. We hate guns. Our parents wouldn't even let us have water guns because they were too violent. We had animal-shaped toys in the bathtub that would squirt water out their mouths for Christ's sake! Lydia doesn't have a gun! This has to be a prop. What an elaborate scene you've created, dark little Lee! You do fucked-up more beautifully than anyone ever did fucked-up. You're an Edward Gorey character. L is for Lydia who Lied about Living.

I couldn't escape this morbid playact. I was trapped in this fucked-up scene, one of two characters: one living, one deceased. I can see myself calling Anna and weeping what happened to her over the phone. And I can see myself trying to process as I stayed on the line while Anna sobbed into her office phone and called the police. I can see me checking Lydia's pulse. And screaming because there's no pulse. I rifled through her closet and I found a pillowcase. I covered her face. I had to cover her face. I shut the door and went downstairs. I let the dogs in the house and I sat on the couch, like an automaton. The dogs licked my face, nervously, they didn't know what was happening. Their kisses snapped me out of it. Another flipped switch. I came rushing back to reality, back to feeling every painful nanosecond. I was no longer a character. I was me again. This was no hoax. No play. This was fucking happening.

I felt like I was losing my mind.

I wailed so loudly the dogs started howling. I began hyperventilating. I couldn't breathe. It was all happening so fast. There was a pounding on the door and police and firefighters and EMTs spilled in. I just sat there silently, pointed them upstairs. Then Anna was there, devastated. My mother arrived soon after, driven by our family friends Joel and Debbie, the same friends who kept me and Lydia when Wade died and we were too young to go to his funeral. They were there for us again. In this our worst hour. My mother looked so scared. So lost. Like a kid. That's the only way to describe the look on her face: uncomprehending, like a terrified child. Like we must have looked all those times growing up when we were so devastated by life.

Is this the world? This can't be the world. Please tell me this is not the world!

Those moments were child's play compared to this.

Neighbors began milling around Lydia's house, wondering what was going on. We retreated inside. We couldn't talk about it, not now. A detective showed up and headed up the staircase. After a while he came back down and confirmed what we already knew. Yes. She is actually dead. Looks like a suicide. They'll do an investigation of course, but . . . he didn't even finish his sentence. Just handed us his card and left. I started hyperventilating again. Everyone said I was in shock. My family wanted me to go to the hospital, to hop in the ambulance with the EMTs, but I managed to calm my breathing. I wasn't going anywhere. I was staying right where I was, for every single step of this. One by one people started leaving. There would be paperwork and investigations and whatever else they told us but for now, they would leave us alone. In our grief. In our destroyed, shitty new world.

A heavy rain moved in, unlike anything we'd had in months. The first rain of that long, hot summer. The first relief I can remember. We sat there in my dead little sister's living room, on the furniture that we would take ourselves or give away or drag out to the alley and abandon in the days to come, and we listened. To the booming thunder. To the pelting of the raindrops on the roof. We didn't say a word. We just listened. To the sound of Lydia's departure.

I went to my house and picked up my dog and headed

over to my parents' house. Anna was already there with her husband, Sam. We sobbed and sobbed and sobbed. Wept until our chests hurt, until our sternums literally ached.

You're saying literally too much.

My father was inside a Guantanamo Bay jail cell when he got the news. He and Anna had joined a group that tries to get wrongfully imprisoned detainees out. The Gitmo Lawyers. Pro bono work. They'd both been down there a number of times by that point. Anna had to make the call to my dad, patched through who knows how many military connections before some jarhead had to pull him aside.

Mr. Holland, you have a call.

He was with his client Ahmed at the time, a man eight years into a post-9/11 detainment, a man my father would eventually spring. Long after that horrible day, my dad told me how Ahmed held him there in that cell, among the soccer magazines and expensive olive oils he had requested my father bring him; how the burden of representation shifted from prisoner to counsel in that moment, humanity over injustice.

"My problems are nothing," he told him. "Go. Go home to your family."

They airlifted my father out. Flew him to Jamaica, then Miami, then on to Denver, alone in his grief for some twenty hours. He was there the next day, the new patriarch of a shattered family. His baby daughter dead and gone.

I was supposed to go to a Rockies game the night of Lydia's death, with the girl I was seeing, Katie. It was a big deal. We hadn't gone on many dates. I was so closed off. But she was trying to get in and I was trying to let her; to stop navel-gazing my way through life like a stand-up comic and share myself instead; learn about someone else for a change. We both loved baseball, our Rockies. We were excited.

I called her up and told her what happened. She was so stunned she couldn't even respond. Later that night she came over to my parents' house. I met her outside, on the street. She'd never met my family. We had barely started dating. This was not the time. But she knew Lydia. She had met her at the Squire open mic a handful of times. And she felt my devastation. I could see it on her face. We walked down Montview to City Park. We walked around the lake, watching the bats fly low over the water spearing insects. We didn't say a word. What was there to say? So I mouthed the only words I could think of, neurotically, over and over and over again, head down, barely paying attention to Katie.

Rest in peace, little doodle.

We staged a beautiful service. In Anna's backyard. We had to police the numbers, the outpouring was so immense. So many were affected by her, enraptured by her. The little genius, suffering muse. Her collection of Colorado Springs misfit friends made the trek, heartbroken. There were more artists and musicians and comics assembled there than I had ever seen in one place. Her best friend Heather, Anna, myself, and my dad all spoke. My mom lay in Anna's bedroom and listened, away from the crowd. That's why we had chosen Anna's house for the service. So my mom could be there without attending. She was so broken she couldn't even stand. She opened the windows so she could hear the eulogies from the second story where she lay in her eldest daughter's bed and listened to the funeral of her youngest. After my remarks I went and lay next to her and we listened to my dad's voice boom over the PA, sounding like some great orator from years past. He went on and on and on, ten pages worth. He had so much to say. Normally we would tease him for being long-winded. That day every word was a gift. We could have listened forever. We smiled at his words; we laughed at his loving descriptions; we cried at his pain, because it was ours.

Lydia's singer-songwriter friend closed the ceremony by singing "Amazing Grace" and playing guitar. We didn't know he was going to; he just broke into it. It so moved my mother that she got out of bed and joined the mourners, left her post in Anna's bed and headed down the stairs and into the backyard. Everyone wanted to hug her, the gutted matriarch, and she graciously received them all. We all took turns holding my nephew Henry and my new niece Sylvie in our arms. We practically fought over them. We needed them so badly in that moment. They helped remind us that this family, this lineage, would move forward. It did not stop here. It was not dead and gone. Even though Lydia was.

Of course the second they left our arms, it was impossible to remember that. It felt like everything was slipping away.

People say the service helped them. It did nothing for me. Funerals are not for the family. They are for the others. Families aren't afforded the luxury of having one place to deposit their grief; there's just too much. Especially with a suicide. It spills out everywhere. It's impossible to contain.

We went out for drinks that night and more people came, those who didn't feel right attending a service that was supposedly just friends and family, but people who wanted to pay their respects nonetheless. I drank with them all. I accepted every one of their shot offers. I did it a lot in the months that followed. We closed down the bar that night, everyone blindly shit-canned, many sobbing. It was like some ferociously tragic scene in a coming-of-age movie that Lydia and I would check out at the Esquire on a Monday at midnight. She would have loved it.

Our in-boxes filled with condolences, our mail slots with letters, our porches with flowers. Someone kept knitting small red hearts and leaving them on our fence posts and doorknobs. It was all so nice, so thoughtful and heartfelt. And none of it helped at all. People wrote little cards and notes and every one just reminded us of a pain we had never forgotten in the first place. Not even for a second. So we just thanked them for their kind thoughts while we lumbered forward broken, trudging through the haze, day after nightmarish day. The Magnificent Cayton-Hollands, down a core member. The best family in the world, now four, not five.

As a creative type you tend to self-mythologize. And in that solipsism it's impossible not to wonder what the point of the whole story is; what it all revolves around, the through-line, the arc. And then one day it hits you like a ton of bricks, like a bullet to your little sister's fucking head: oh, *this* is it. This is what the story has been all about. All that time you spent thinking it revolved around you, you weren't even the main character, you idiot.

She was.

And now she's gone.

So you walk around, lesser, with a giant void inside of yourself and you pray that you can close the book on this story soon and move on to another. Which, of course, you can't. Because this *is* the story. The only story. What happened to Lydia, that's your cornerstone, the event around which you now calibrate yourself, your narrative. Your family's narrative. All your stories are linked to this one, irrevocably. Everything that happens to you from here on out, it will always come back to this new horrific truth. It will always be a story of how the world became a sadder, crueler place for you. Your life will forever be viewed through a lens of profound absence.

Until the day you join her on the other side.

MEMORIES WITHOUT HER

We rented a house outside Fort Collins soon after Lydia died, in Roosevelt National Forest, near the Red Feather Lakes. We had to do something. We were just barely limping along. It was important to try to make new memories together as a family, memories without her. That's what one of the shrinks my parents went to suggested anyway. That we start building up new experiences without the deceased as soon as possible. As if we had a choice. Every experience since July 31, 2012, was without the deceased. Every night I sobbed until my rib cage hurt; every time I instinctively went to call her and see what she was up to and remembered *Oh yeah*. All I had done was rack up memories without Lydia, memories I didn't want. I didn't see how sitting in a house together with the nuclear unit minus one was going to do anything to help us move past Lydia's suicide. But here we were.

This is what broken families do. One foot in front of the other. Rent a mountain house. Cook meals together. Sit in the hot tub. Play Trivial Pursuit. Attempt normalcy.

Anna brought Sam and her two kiddos, Henry and Sylvie. Henry was three at the time. Sylvie was not even six months old. Sam had offered to keep the kids, to let his wife go be with her brother and parents and grieve, but Anna wanted them there. This experience involved them too whether we liked it or not; this was now a plot twist in their narratives as well. The ghost of Aunt Lydia. Mom's sister. Henry was cognizant of what was happening. They had to explain death to him, the same way my parents had to help me with those starving African children in the commercials. And Sylvie felt the weight of the blow whether she knew it or not. After Lydia's death Anna could barely produce enough breast milk to feed her baby. She was too weak.

The house was beautiful, with a huge deck that looked out over an enormous rock outcropping, from the top of which you could see all the way to Wyoming. You could see all the damage from the recent fires. We climbed it every day, mostly myself and Sam, but sometimes my dad too. After we became more familiar with the terrain, Sam decided Henry should come with us. It wasn't all that difficult and Sam would bring along the baby carrier so he could throw Henry on his back if need be. Anna was nervous about the idea, understandably overprotective. Sam politely insisted. It would be fine. We set off together through the grasslands one morning, Henry excited to be out there with the defining men of his young existence: Papi, Dad, Uncle Adam. My mom and Anna called after him from the deck. He looked back at them, blowing on their steaming mugs of coffee and tea. They were waving at him, smiling. Henry laughed and waved back.

When we were kids my aunt and uncle and cousins came out to visit from Virginia and we took them up to Rocky Mountain National Park for the day. We had a picnic lunch in a remote field deep in the park, and when Lydia was done she asked if she could go play. My mom told her to stay where we could see her. Lydia said she would, but after a while she headed off toward a small cluster of trees on the far side of the clearing; they were all huddled out in front of the wall of the forest, like a portico into the woods. My mom yelled at her to turn around and come back but Lydia either couldn't hear her or pretended not to. She was exploring.

"Goddamn it," my mom said. "What's the one thing I told her not to do?"

From the far side of the clearing, to our right, we noticed movement. One by one a herd of elk emerged from the woods. There must have been two dozen, led by two impressive males. It was almost mating season, when visitors flock to the park to witness the iconic bugling of the Rocky Mountain elk. It's also when the animals are at their most dangerous. Not a year went by that you didn't hear about some dumb tourist in Estes Park getting charged or trampled or gored because they got too close. Now a herd of them was heading directly for Lydia. We tried to distract them, to veer them off their course. We stood up and yelled and waved our hands. But they were steadfast.

They continued along their path undeterred, eventually disappearing into the small thicket that contained my little sister. We went silent, held our breath. We listened for sounds of . . . anything. Time moved so slowly. Then the first elk emerged on the other side of the grove, then the next, finally the entire heard. Once they were safely out of sight, Lydia emerged from the cluster of trees as well, from the opposite side that the elk had exited. She ran to us as fast as she could.

"What is wrong with you?" my mom yelled. "I told you to stay close!"

"That was incredible!" Lydia said, gasping, out of breath.

She had been exploring when she heard a branch snap. She looked up and saw the first elk, not twenty feet away. It huffed, alarmed by her presence. It had not expected to see a little girl in the woods, nor Lydia an elk. Yet there they were: sudden new acquaintances. Then Lydia noticed the other elk behind the first, all completely still, watching her. She said they seemed on edge. These elk had no doubt seen humans before, maybe even humans with weapons. They were sizing her up. Calmly but as quickly as she could, Lydia climbed up a tree until she sat on a branch, far above them. They eyed her dubiously, but eventually determined she wasn't a threat. They continued along their way cautiously, beneath Lydia's dangling feet. She watched them go, breathless. And then they disappeared from her field of vision, a memory, a magic moment in the woods.

My mom tried to act mad, but we were all as amazed by Lydia's story as she was. We listened to every detail, rapt. Just like we did for Henry when he returned safely from his big hike with the men, babbling excitedly about prickly pear and wildflowers, butterflies and grasshoppers.

I found Henry that night in the house, wandering around, confused. He was crying. He had gotten up in the middle of the night and didn't know where he was. And he was terrified. I was asleep on the foldout couch in the living room.

"Rooster, what's the matter buddy?" They'd started calling him that in the womb: Rooster. He came out with red hair and it stuck. Poor little Rooster Dooster, wailing in the strange, dark cabin.

I picked him up in my arms and he sobbed into my chest, clutching me tightly, trembling. I carried him downstairs to the basement room where Anna and Sam and Sylvie were all sleeping. I shook Anna awake by the shoulder. She snapped to.

"He wandered upstairs and didn't know where he was, the poor thing," I explained, lowering my nephew down into my one living sister's arms.

"Come here, baby," Anna cooed.

She took him from my arms and pulled him against her, his face buried in the nape of her neck. She whispered *thank you* to me and faded off back to sleep with her family, intact there in that basement, safe and warm.

You're fine, Rooster Dooster, I wanted to whisper to

him. Never mind the strange shadows in the night. Never mind the darkness that's always waiting there, just around the corner. Don't concern yourself with that. We're not going to let anything bad happen to you. You hear me? We're the Magnificent Cayton-Hollands. And you're one of us now. And yes Aunt Lydia is gone but you don't worry about that now, buddy. That pain is not for you. That's for us. Let it go. You just sleep next to your mom and your dad and your sister and know that you're going to be okay because we're looking out for you, from now until forever. Now more than ever before. Trust me, Henry, nothing bad is going to happen. Not again. We won't let it. I won't let it. I promise.

I'd whispered similar words to myself as a child, when Lydia almost drowned. I wondered if Henry knew they meant nothing now.

The next morning, after breakfast, something was off. It was too quiet.

"Where's Flannery?" my mom asked me.

"I don't know," I said. "Where's Annabel?"

Our Chesapeake Bay retrievers were missing, mine and my mom's. They're sisters, both from the same litter. My mom owned their mother, Sylvia. She was the best dog we ever had. So my mom bred her. There were seven puppies. I took Annabel. My mom took Flannery. They love each other. Best-friend sissies. That's how we refer to them in our dumb dog-voices. *Best-friend sissies.*

And now they were missing.

We sprung into emergency mode, panicked. Of course we assumed the worst. That was all any of us could do anymore. That was our collective mind-set. Two missed calls from dad?! Someone's dead! Mom not answering the phone?! She fell down the stairs. She's hurt. Something's wrong. Something's terribly wrong.

We searched the house and found a tear in the screen door in the basement. Annabel and Flannery had barreled through it. Best-friend sissies gone exploring. We searched for the next hour but couldn't find them. I could sense that my mom was on the cusp of a breakdown. Maybe I was just projecting. I felt like I couldn't breathe. Not my dog. Not Annabel. Please God I can't take anymore. Anna's dog Belden died shortly after Lydia. It was too much. Death was coming at our family from all sides. Why did this keep happening?

We speculated that maybe some coyotes had herded our dogs off and then turned on them. Or what if they had encountered a mountain lion, or black bear? We gathered on the porch and tried to act rational. Formulate a plan of attack. Call the park ranger, Google the closest shelters, make missing animal posters.

Then we noticed movement, on the horizon, like the elk in Rocky Mountain National Park, but smaller, faster, fewer of them. Annabel and Flannery, back from an adventure, tails wagging. We called out to them and they came running as fast as they could, happy to be back in their safe spaces. They smiled those guilty Chessie smiles, lips curled up above their goofy teeth. They knew they had done wrong. When they finally reached the porch we went to embrace them only to be hit by the sheer force of their smell. It was putrid. They had gotten into something foul.

"Good god!" I said. "What, did they roll around in shit somewhere? Do you think they went to those horse stables?"

"That's not horse shit," my mom said. "That's something dead."

They had found a carcass out on the land around the house, some deer or fox or raccoon and gone to town in its remains. Canine ecstasy: backs on the ground, legs up in the air, gyrating, rubbing it in deep. Doggie heaven. And they reeked.

We got out the hose and sprayed them down, sponged their chests and bellies and legs as best we could, but it hardly had any effect. A couple hours later, same routine, same result. They just stank, no two ways about it. Whatever it was had saturated them. It would take days for the smell of death to leave them. They were covered in it. We all were.

THE GRIEF PEDDLER

Ten days after Lydia died I went to Los Angeles for my as-previously-scheduled post-Montreal victory lap. Like everything was somehow normal. Like that's just what you do. Go kick some ass in Montreal, come home to bear witness to your little sister's suicide, head off to Hollywood to try to maintain that heat! All part of the game.

I didn't want to go. I was having trouble putting one foot in front of the other. I kept having nightmares: me walking into Lydia's house, then up the stairs, through the doorway, until . . . the end. I drank myself to sleep every night, tried to knock myself out cold so I wouldn't dream at all. But then I could barely get out of bed the next morning. My dog had to howl to rouse me. And then of course there were the flashbacks that seemingly came at random: driving, jogging around the park, in line for a burrito. There was nothing I could do about those. Hardly the time to go to Hollywood and chase the dream. But my family insisted I make the trip. Lydia would have wanted that, they said. She was my biggest cheerleader. She would be devastated if her death derailed all the progress I had made.

Like I gave a fuck. I was still too mad at Lydia to care what she would have wanted. But I could sense that my family needed it, and I suppose I did too. We needed a distraction, a break from the relentless misery that was consuming us. And if I could provide that in even some small way, I felt like I probably should. Every minute I was discussing Hollywood douchebaggery was another minute we weren't all talking about death.

I told my manager to not set me up with any meaningless meetings. I was hanging on by a frayed thread; my threshold for bullshit was nil. He assured me that he would do his best. And if I felt overwhelmed or like I couldn't maintain, he told me to just get up and walk out. I had nothing to prove to anyone.

So I shuttled from meeting to meeting, from general to general, from the Sony lot to CBS Radford, from Warner Bros. to Comedy Central, hundreds of meaningless miles racked up in a rental car as the strip malls of Los Angeles blurred together through the tears streaming down my face.

Some of the people I met with were the same people I had rubbed shoulders with in Montreal two weeks before, thousands of miles away, a lifetime ago.

"Adam!" they'd exclaim when I walked into the room, my black-and-white headshot sitting on the desk in front of them. "How's it going, man! What have you been up to since Montreal?!"

Finding my little sister's body, writing her eulogy, holding my mother while she weeps.

"Uh-huh, uh-huh, that's great! Listen, we are going to keep you in mind for *anything* that comes up. We've got our eye on you!"

At night I drank alone until I felt numb. Then I'd head out on foot. I never had a destination in mind, it just felt good to move. To remember that I was alive. That my limbs were working and could carry me in whatever direction I chose. I'd make turns down streets I didn't recognize. I'd deliberately try to get lost. And when the neighborhood would inevitably turn seedy or dangerous, I embraced it. Like a lunatic. I would start talking to God through gritted teeth, quietly, beneath my breath. I would goad him, dare him to do his worst.

Go ahead, fuck with me. Do it. I want you too. Bring the darkness down upon me. I fucking dare you.

I was so full of hurt and rage that if anyone or anything tried to harass me I would have exploded. I felt like I could destroy anything I came up against. And I wanted to. I wanted to destroy it all. And should I come up against some force that I couldn't take out, well then let it take me. Let this all come to an end. At least then Lydia and I would be together again, like pieces of popcorn on a movie theater floor.

But nothing ever came for me. God, the darkness, whatever forces pulse all around us, they lay dormant, satiated, belly full. They'd gotten all they needed from me, from my family. Cowards.

I kept going to meetings. Including one with Amazon.

They liked our script enough to give us money to make a pilot. In Denver. Just like I always wanted. So there was that. I called home and let my family know. They were thrilled. And proud. I had sold a TV show. This was a worthy distraction. The trip could be called a success.

I was elated. And I didn't care at all.

Before I went back home, a girl I went to high school with messaged me out of the blue. She was living in Los Angeles and had heard the news about Lydia. She said she was heading out to a friend's beach house in Malibu for the day and wondered if I wanted to join. It was such a kind, unexpected offer I couldn't even think of a reason to say no. I just accepted. When I showed up my friend hadn't arrived yet. Some guy I had never met answered the door of a massive house, right on the water.

"You must be Adam," he said with a smile.

I wondered what all he knew, what my friend had told him. Did he know me as Adam the comic, a funny friend from Denver visiting LA? Or was I Adam the guy whose little sister just killed herself? Adam the broken? Was there even a difference anymore?

He toured me around his house and then neither one of us really knew what to say. We just stood there in silence, both wishing our mutual friend would show up.

"You can go swimming if you want," he offered. "I just got out, but if you feel like hopping in the ocean, by all means."

I headed down to the private beach, a little swath of Malibu all to myself. The water was freezing so I made my way in cautiously, as if slowly absorbing the cold would somehow mitigate it. But it never does. Best to take it all on at once. I gave up and dove under the brackish waves, swimming as fast as I could to warm my body. Soon my feet no longer touched the bottom and I stopped swimming and just floated there, a tiny head bobbing on the surface of the water.

I took it all in: the surfers to my left seated on their boards waiting for the perfect waves, the rows of houses behind me, all glass and sleek, modern lines. I watched two brothers on the shore try to throw a regulation football that their little hands were far too tiny to grip. Overhead, column after column of pelicans approached, then disappeared down the beach. I tried to appreciate it all in the way my dad had taught me when I was a kid, to marvel at the beauty of the world and the miraculous turn of events that allowed me to ever be here in the first place. But I couldn't. I couldn't see any beauty. I couldn't feel any wonder. Everything felt hollow. I didn't belong there, or anywhere. I tried to sink. Tucked my knees into my chest and dropped to the ocean floor. I closed my eyes and tried to feel the water take me in whatever direction it thought I should go. I wondered if it would suck me out to sea, the way it did Wade and Lincoln all those years ago, back when the darkness first crept into our sunny little lives. But it didn't. It wanted nothing to do with me. It just kept pushing me up to the surface. I was drowning. And I was so very much alive.

THOSE WHO CAN'T

Those Who Can't saved my life. Temporarily, anyway. It made me want to continue living it. If only to see what would happen. I had spent the last eight years chasing stand-up comedy. Then my little sister died. Suddenly my act felt false. Like getting up onstage and not talking about Lydia was somehow a betrayal—to myself, to the medium. And yet to try to mine humor from what happened felt callous and cheap. What, was I going to unload a hot ten minutes about my sister's suicide while dudes in trucker hats sucked down buckets of overpriced Bud Lights? Making a pilot was something else entirely. Something new. And *Those Who Can't* wasn't just my baby. It was also Ben and Andrew's. It was not just a reflection of me. It was a reflection of the Grawlix. Which meant I didn't have to feel guilty for not addressing what I was thinking about every day. This was not the place for that. This was a TV show about bad teachers. I could leave all the Lydia baggage behind.

It also represented the biggest career opportunity of my life. If we knocked this pilot out of the park, there was the promise of more. A TV show that we created, wrote, and starred in loomed on our horizon. We just had to execute. And I wanted that. In spite of everything I wanted to rise to the occasion, not mourn alongside it while it passed me by.

We called in every favor we could. We reached out to every talented person we knew in Denver to help. Our friends designed and dressed the set, they did our hair and makeup, our wardrobe, actors lent their services, local businesses donated food. A few of our funniest comedy buddies from LA flew out to play our fellow teachers in the fictional school. The Nix Brothers directed. It remains to this day the single most fulfilling creative experience I have ever had. We took no pay. We channeled every cent of the $50,000 budget into the production.

And it was fun. A fucking blast, actually. Which was such a relief. At that point in my life I wasn't even sure if I could have fun anymore. I often forbade myself to. But there I was on set, laughing harder than I ever had, right alongside everyone else. Like one of the gang. Like nothing had changed. To be experiencing that much joy gave me the first glimmer of hope for my future. I was enjoying myself. And I was operating on a high comedic level. Realizing that I could do both of those things in the wake of Lydia's death was revelatory.

Anna, my mom, and my dad were regular visitors on set that week. I think the buzz of it helped us all through those first few months. *Adam and his friends are making a TV show.* It was something new and exciting in the midst of everything new and heartbreaking.

I fooled myself into thinking, *If I can just pour my grief into this, then everything will be okay.*

Inevitably it spilled out, though. I couldn't always contain it.

I went to my neighborhood bar alone one night. A friend of a friend approached me and asked if he could join. He knew what had happened and he shared that his brother also killed himself. We closed the bar down together. I let it all out, to this virtual stranger. We talked about it from every angle—the guilt, the anger, the sadness. The fear that from now on people will view you as somehow damaged, lesser. Or worse, pity you. We guzzled alcohol and mined our heartbreak like characters from some overwrought play. And it felt great. Like a catharsis. The next morning, I woke up to a pounding hangover and a Facebook message from the guy.

"Nice hanging, man," it read. "Let's do it again some time and we'll both try and act less emo."

It was funny. And nice. A perfectly appropriate gesture from a kind soul who could sympathize. I immediately deleted it. I felt ashamed, like I had done something inappropriate, like the whole experience had been some sordid, emotional one-night stand that I couldn't put in the rearview mirror fast enough. I had done nothing wrong. He had done nothing wrong. But I was flailing. And that embarrassed me. I like to maintain control. And that night I had spun out. I chose not to interpret it as a sign of some larger need to address what was going on with me. Just like I was ignoring the flashbacks and nightmares I kept having, or my inability to accept that Lydia had killed herself. I kept calling the lead detective after the case had been closed, asking him new questions I had thought of, pointing out new leads that could indicate foul play. Only when he half threatened to walk me through the graphic crime scene photos to prove it was a suicide did I back off. And yet I didn't heed any of those warning signs that I was coming unglued. I just kept working on *Those Who Can't*.

We filmed a couple of scenes at my and Lydia's alma mater, East High School. It filled me with immense pride to be walking down Rivera Hall, the one named after the beloved newspaper sponsor, who had passed away. I thought about him looking down on me. How proud he would be. I pictured Lydia right by his side. She was no doubt proud of me too. It felt good to think of her that way: proud, cognizant of what I was doing, enjoying the fruits of my labor. I started to see them as the fruits of *our* labor. I was overcompensating but I ran with it.

Lydia had very little to do with *Those Who Can't*. But in my head she was carrying the production. I was entering a period of mourning where I was taking her on my back. Any career success I achieved, it was going to be for her, with her, of her. I was living for two now. Lydia had only gotten twenty-eight years; I was going to live out the rest for the both of us. Which meant I had to work twice as hard, succeed twice as hard, live twice as hard. It was meathead philosophy but it felt good, and right. Like a big brother ought to do. You couldn't fix her or save her while she was here? Time to suck the marrow out of life in her absence. She didn't get to so you damn well better. Not just for you, for her. Especially for her. And in *Those Who Can't* it felt like I may just be doing that. I was fulfilling our mutual comedy-nerd fantasy.

Then we wrapped. And the next morning I flew to North Carolina, where we were meeting my aunt and uncle and cousins for Thanksgiving at a rental house on the Outer Banks. Seemed like a good time to get the extended family together, away from our dining room and Lydia's empty chair. It was the first break I had taken since selling the script. My parents were already there. Anna, as was her custom, would be with her husband's family in Nebraska. So, painfully hungover after the wrap party the night before, I boarded a plane, alone, took my seat, and thought, *Well now what?*

I didn't know. Since Lydia died in July I had been breathing *Those Who Can't*. I was obsessed with it, every detail of the script and preproduction, then production. But now, some five months later, it was done. We would have to edit it, sure, but postproduction was weeks away. And then we would have to wait and see what became of it, what Mother Amazon held in store, seedlings of hoped parsed out over the next few months and coming year. But that was all in the future. In the interim, there was the now—the blank, sudden now. And the reality of all that happened set in like it hadn't since those first few weeks after her death. Things came back into focus and I was staring at the bleakness of my life again, at this unimaginable future. It was so terrifyingly unfamiliar. What was this place, this desolate, new landscape? For the previous thirty-two years it had been one thing, now it was something else entirely. It was like a limb had been chopped off, but I could still feel it. Lydia the phantom.

My parents bought me a first-class flight as a gift for a job well done on *Those Who Can't*, and I promptly began sobbing as breakfast was served. The fifteen white men in the cabin around me didn't know what to make of it. They fidgeted in their seats uncomfortably as they ate their omelets. They hadn't been privy to this type of raw heartbreak since Obama was elected.

My cousin Molly's boyfriend Mone came along with the family to North Carolina. They had been together for a few years. The first night there Mone pulled me aside and shared he was going to ask Molly to marry him. He was nervous and giddy. The next morning, we all watched from the balcony as it happened. He took her down to the beach, far from our prying eyes, until they were just two tiny figures on the shore. Then one figure was kneeling down on his knee in the sand. And then they were two figures embracing. Everyone on the balcony cheered, myself included, but inside I seethed. I had never been more jealous in my life. Not for me, for Lydia. Because she would never get a moment like this. That wasn't fair. Why didn't she get to experience that high?

And I felt so ashamed for being so jealous. I loved Molly like a sister; we had grown up together. This was my flesh and blood and I couldn't be happy for her? What the fuck was wrong with me? My empathy had vanished. My capacity for joy was nonexistent. I looked at my dad and my mom there on that balcony, sipping celebratory mimosas, smiling. They were so happy for Molly, but I could tell they felt it too. I could see it on their faces. They would never get to share this with their youngest daughter.

That night my uncle Lauren built a bonfire on the beach and we all got drunk. I was the first to head down to the beach to join him. We drank and listened to the Atlantic pound the shore. A recent hurricane had cleared out the area. It had been difficult to get there but it was worth it. We had the entire place to ourselves. Not another person on the beach, except for us, two Caytons pondering the void. Eventually Lauren's wife, Maynee, came down from the house, then my cousin Griffin, followed by the lovebirds Molly and Mone. We all wrapped blankets around ourselves and nestled down into the sand by the fire.

My parents were the last to join. By the time they ventured out they were both well on their way. They walked arm in arm, each drunkenly supporting the other. A thin, wood-plank walkway led over the dunes to the beach. As my parents stepped from the walkway down into the sand, they took a spill, clumsily navigating the surface change. The two of them toppled over and we all burst out laughing. Which they did as well. They laughed long and hard.

Then they tried to get up but couldn't because they were too shit-canned, too hopelessly stuck in the sand. And they just kept laughing at their dumb, drunk fate. It was the first time I had heard them laugh together since Lydia had died. It was the first time I had seen them smiling together. They had been through so much; the feelings of guilt I was feeling, they were tenfold for my parents. They were grieving in polar opposite ways; my mother retreating inward, my father bursting to talk about it. Most of the time they seemed on different pages. And here they were, like drunk teenagers in the sand, cackling. Happy. It was too much. I turned toward the ocean and walked toward the water, not sure if I was ever going to stop, tears streaming down my face. I wanted the ocean to take me away, just like I had in LA. But I couldn't jump in. Then my family would know something was wrong. And I didn't want to let them in. I didn't want them to see me losing it. I wanted them to just enjoy this moment, to keep on laughing. I wanted them to laugh forever.

I needed help. I couldn't do this by myself anymore.

DESENSITIZATION
AND REPROCESSING

Three weeks later I was in a shitty hotel on the side of the highway in Grand Rapids, Michigan. I had just headlined three shows at Dr. Grins on a Saturday, 6:30, 8:30, 10:30. That 10:30 show broke me. I had a migraine in the green-room minutes before the show started. The white flashes crept into my periphery and I knew one was coming but I didn't feel like there was anything I could do about it. This was my first time at the club, I was new to headlining nationally in general, and I didn't want the word to get out that I was some head case. That I was too sickly to be relied upon. I already worried about what people knew about me, what they knew about Lydia. I worried that they saw me as some depressed ticking time bomb, capable of a tight 45 but bound to unload on an audience onstage one night.

Was that the kind of comic anyone wanted to book?

I was projecting. Bookers checked out my clips and my bio bullet points, maybe. They didn't flesh out my back-story; they didn't debate the state of my psyche. But I didn't know any of that. I just knew I was in the throes of a migraine and I didn't want to disappoint.

The flashes of light in front of my eyes crept outward, then disappeared, as they always do; then my vision was restored but the pain began to nest. It feels like someone cracked you in the forehead with a tree branch. The ache starts in the temple and cascades all the way back to your cerebral cortex. Your head pounds, like the worst hangover you've ever had, except all centralized in your brain. I ordered a beer to the greenroom and pounded it. I ordered another and took it to the stage with me. I drank three more during the course of my set. I invited the audience to join in my debauchery, played the Saturday late-show party guy, but I was just trying to numb the pain in my skull, to punch that migraine right back. I did it. I did my time and survived. I got offstage and headed back to the hotel immediately. No sitting by the exit and thanking the audience for coming, no carousing with the other comics on the bill. I just wanted to sleep. I wasn't even drunk. The migraine and the alcohol had met in the middle and both collapsed. I just hurt.

Back in my hotel room, I sat on the edge of my bed and looked out the window at the cars on the highway speeding past in the dark. I felt so flat, so muted. I felt incapable of experiencing joy, like I didn't deserve to anymore. I had broken up with my girlfriend Katie after Thanksgiving for that exact reason. I made up excuses for why, but the truth was I felt like I wasn't dedicating enough time to suffering. So I selfishly cut her loose. I had to experience this pain with the totality of myself—not with some part of me hoping for a future with a wife and kids, but with all of me miserable, all of me feeling every last drop.

It was more than I had bargained for. It was taking over. I felt done, over it all, more depressed than I had ever been. For the first time since college I wanted to kill myself. But I couldn't even do that. I couldn't take my own life, couldn't join Lydia on the other side. I had seen firsthand what that does to a family. Lydia had shown me and in showing me she had removed the choice, forever. I could never do that to my mom and my dad, to Anna and Henry and Sylvie. Never. No matter how low I was feeling, they didn't deserve to experience something like that. Again. The new realization made me feel trapped. Because as bad as things got, as miserable as I was right there in that hotel room, I could never escape it even if I wanted to. There was no out for me, no end to this. I crawled beneath the comforter and sobbed loud and long, gasping for breath that wasn't there.

The phone rang on the bedside table.

"Mr. Clayton-Holland?"

They never get my name right. Everyone adds a phantom "L" to Cayton. Everyone.

"Yes?" I said, not even bothering to correct them.

"We got a call about a disturbance coming from your room."

"You did?"

"Yeah. Is someone crying in there?"

"Oh," I said embarrassed. "I'm sorry. That was me. I'll be quiet."

The front deskman didn't know what to say.

"Are you okay?" he stammered.

I thought about the question, then answered truthfully. "No."

I had been bouncing from shrink to shrink since Lydia had died, hating all of them. I'd find various reasons for rejecting them. Most of their offices were located in sad, suburban office parks. If these were the type of insipid spaces they chose to conduct their businesses from, to spend their professional lives in, could I really trust them with my psychological well-being? Anna, for her part, critiqued her various shrinks based on their décor. Was some indigenous office art too goddamn much to ask?

We sounded like Lydia.

At an annual physical with my doctor he asked me about my emotional state. I told him the truth. Not good. He asked if I had heard of EMDR. I had not.

Eye Movement Desensitization and Reprocessing is an aggressive form of treatment used to help trauma victims, such as soldiers, affected by PTSD. But it can help anyone who's been through some shit. I gave it a try. As I sat with my new therapist on my initial intake she listened patiently and thoughtfully to my sob story, but kept her distance. With all the other shrinks I felt this immense sense of pity. It was cloying. They flinched and sighed dramatically with every detail of my story; they emoted and tried to show me how sympathetic they were. And I resented it. I was tired of people feeling sorry for me. I didn't need compassion. I needed help. This new doctor seemed relatively nonplussed. She wasn't unsympathetic, she said the appropriate things, but her attitude was one of yeah, fucked-up things happen, let's get to treating them. I would later learn that she's a leading expert in the field, that she regularly works with people who have been sexually abused their entire lives, or tortured. And that she had suffered some trauma herself. My case was a sad one, but not the worst story she had ever heard, not in the least.

I needed that. To not be babied. To be reminded that suffering is a huge part of the world, something that doesn't need coddling, but treatment. And so we began our therapy.

"It helps to try to envision the human brain as a filing cabinet," she said. "The memory of finding Lydia dead that day has become like a loose file, one that keeps coming up at inappropriate times in the form of nightmares and flashbacks. EMDR is a way of filing that memory away, so that it's there to access should you chose to access it, but it remains in a fixed, secure location until that point."

Sold.

I sat in an oversized armchair in her tastefully appointed, centrally located office, closed my eyes, and went through the morning that I found Lydia, in painful, intimate detail. My therapist pushed and prodded me through it, urging me to recall every last thing. She kept asking questions.

What did the dogs sound like in the backyard? Was

the light on or off in the upstairs hallway? Did the sun-rays come in through the window of Lydia's bedroom that morning?

While I answered her I clenched two buttons in my fists that pulsed electronically back and forth, left then right, left then right, like a metronome. This was meant to simu-late REM (rapid eye movement), the state in which we best process information. My brain was essentially acting as it would if I were asleep. I was awake, dreaming.

The process of EMDR can fast prove overwhelming so the patient must determine a happy place to retreat to when it all gets to be too much. I chose a sand dune in Cape Cod.

We lived there for a summer. I was twelve, Lydia eight. Anna was fourteen. Her figure skating was taking off. So much so that Nancy Kerrigan's coach had agreed to train her, provided we make our way out to the Cape for the summer. So we did. Packed up the cars and moved the fam-ily out to Chatham for three glorious months. It was noth-ing but baseball and fireworks, cranberries and swimming every day. And when I wasn't doing that I was at the skat-ing rink heartsick in love with Nancy Kerrigan. She wasn't yet plagued by her run-in with that trollop Tonya Hard-ing, she was just herself, Olympics bound, stunning and elegant, all legs and skates and teeth. A beautiful goddamn thoroughbred out there on the ice. It was the best summer of my life.

So when the EMDR became too much, my shrink would guide me back to that happy place and make me tell her about it, with the same level of detail and precision that I had talked about finding Lydia. I told her how I could see the ocean in front of me, hear the waves crashing on the shore. I explained how I could feel the house we had rented behind me, with my family in it, and I knew that everyone was in there, safe and happy and alive. I could sense it. I painted the image of me out there on that dune, listening to the wind through the reeds and feeling it on my skin, the saltwater and the sand. Everything felt tranquil. Everything was right in the world.

And then the session was over.

She cautioned me that the experience could be staggering but after that first EMDR session, I felt like I was on drugs. Sounds were louder, lights were brighter, smells were more intense. All stimuli came in full bore. I felt as if every receptor in my entire body was more open and attuned to the universe, like someone had stuck a master key in my brain, twisted it, and now all the doors were open. I wandered around the neighborhood for an hour before I felt comfortable driving home. I felt altered, like I was viewing the world in an entirely different way.

EMDR was the best mushrooms I ever ate. It was also the most expensive.

What was amazing about each session was how new details would emerge. There was nothing different about the treatment, it was the same exact process every time, but the memories became clearer. My brain was changing. I saw that morning from new angles, remembered tiny, insignificant details. What her cats were doing. What Lydia was wearing. Her laptop on the bedside table. The picture crystalized even further. Which was painful, but necessary. I needed to see it all before I could file it away. It had to be absolutely vivid. I began to crave going in for EMDR. As hard as it was, as much as I cried and hated revisiting the most painful experience of my life on a routine basis, something about the process satisfied me. It spoke to my obsessive-compulsion. It was rote and methodical, the same exact thing every time, the only variant my brain. When I grabbed those electronic pulses in my fists, and my therapist turned on the machine so that they would tick-tock back and forth, I couldn't help but summon my old bedtime routine.

04-09, 04-09, 04-09, 04-09, 04-09, 04-09, 04-09, 04.

My toes are relaxed, my feet are relaxed, my ankles and Achilles tendons and shins are relaxed.

And it worked. We did eight, nine, maybe ten sessions, I can't really remember. But at some point I had just had enough. I didn't want to go over Lydia's death anymore. The memory felt sufficiently processed. I was done with it. I didn't need to re-create it again. And it was no longer coming up inappropriately. After the third or fourth session the flashbacks and nightmares dried up. There would be glimmers of them: a hint of the memory, a frame from that horrible scene in the movie playing in my dream, but it was far better than it had been. The memory was filing itself away. I felt like I was starting to control it. Which was freeing. To not be plagued by it. It was there, and I brought it back out of the filing cabinet often. But I got to choose when I did.

Shortly after stopping EMDR I had a dream. I was in my happy place, the sand dune in Cape Cod. I watched the waves lap against the shore, listened to the cry of the seagulls. I could feel the wind through the reeds on my skin. I knew that my family was safe in the house behind me. I could sense it. Everything was as it should be. Everything was calm and quiet. Then I felt a presence sitting next to me. Lydia. Not eight-year-old Lydia. Grown-up Lydia. Twenty-eight-year-old Lydia. Happy and well. Beautiful. She smiled at me. I smiled back. We both turned and stared out over the water together, toward the old world where our ancestors came from, far across the sea. Brother and sister, side by side. Alive.

I LIKE TO REMEMBER
HER CONSTANTLY; I TRY NOT
TO THINK OF HER AT ALL

I started writing about Lydia. I had to. I wasn't talking about her onstage, and the desire to express my feelings about everything that happened was overwhelming me. I felt like my continued silence was a roadblock to my creativity. And yes, I'm aware of how fucking pretentious that sounds, but stand-up comics are allowed to write sentences like that. We're insufferable.

I wrote out of necessity more than anything. I had spent the last eight years of my life in the public sphere, the Denver version of it anyway. But always growing outward. And now, after the defining moment of my life, I was silent. I needed to talk about it in a public way. Call it vanity, call it mourning. I felt like I really didn't have a choice. Plus, some part of me sensed that if I put my thoughts down in a public sphere, I would no longer feel guilty for not talking about it onstage. Because I would have this signature piece that I could point people to.

See, everyone?! I've dealt with it. I'm not hiding from it creatively.

Of course, no one was accusing me of anything remotely like that. Everyone was just letting me mourn however I needed to. But I was feeling that pressure. Every fucking day. So I sat down and penned a screed about all that I had gone through. It was the most painful thing I had ever written. But it felt so cathartic, as beneficial as any therapy or EMDR.

I put the piece out on my website. I hit publish and immediately felt this enormous emotional purge. Like something shifted in me. It was done with. I had talked about what happened. I had incorporated it in some small way into my creative world. That inner pressure I had been putting on myself vanished.

I shared the piece online and drove into the mountains for a hike. I needed to clear my head. I left my phone in the car. Left it all behind for a few hours. When I got back there were hundreds upon hundreds of responses. My comic and writer friends had spread the piece widely across the internet, share after share, retweet after retweet. The reaction was immense and immediate. My inbox filled with touching messages from people who had similarly awful experiences, or had known someone who had. Mostly they thanked me for sharing and told me that it helped them in some small way. One girl wrote that it literally saved her life. That she could see herself in Lydia, could see her family in the depiction of my family, and that she didn't want to do to her family what Lydia had done to ours. I didn't know how to feel about that. Of course I was happy some stranger on the internet had not killed themselves because of something I put out there, but all it really made me think was *lucky you*. Lucky family. I wish my family was so lucky. I wish Lydia had read an article like you did and saved herself.

I had no idea how to deal with the reaction I got. Despite wearing my heart on my sleeve as a child, as I grew older I became more reserved. Grief, despair, those were personal and private. Overt displays of emotion embarrassed me. That's why I turned away at the beach in North Carolina to cry. That's why I kept it together until I reached my hotel room in Grand Rapids. This thing I was carrying around with me was *my* burden. I didn't need any outside observers. At the same time, I had to share it because to not do so felt so dishonest. Maybe this was because I am a Gemini. Maybe it was because my mother was a dry introvert while my father was the most outgoing person in the room. Maybe that's why after spouting off for forty-five minutes from a stage like the life of the goddamn party, I have the hardest time making small talk with anyone that comes up to me. I want every eye in the room on me and then I want everyone to leave me alone. The same was true of what I was writing about Lydia. I wanted everyone to know how I felt but I also didn't want to talk to anyone about it. I certainly didn't want to commiserate. I wasn't trying to take on any more suffering.

And yet suddenly I couldn't shut up about Lydia. I talked about her in storytelling shows. Not stand-up, per se, but closer. I started my own podcast, *My Dining Room Table*. Which was Lydia's dining room table that I inherited. Or took. There was no will. I just moved it to my house. And started broadcasting to the world from it, or at least a couple thousand listeners a week. While that podcast was initially a means for me to interview creative people I found interesting, it quickly became an outlet for me to talk about Lydia. Every few episodes the conversation would inevitably pivot that way, and discussing it openly felt not only right, but necessary. Meanwhile I kept writing, continued publishing pieces on my website and in magazines. And people kept reaching out to me, in larger numbers than ever before.

I started responding to them.

At first I was terrified I would say the wrong thing. But I couldn't just ignore them. So I began firing off a different answer based on how I was feeling at the exact moment.

I like to remember her constantly; I try not to think of her at all.

I focus on helping my family members; I avoid them for weeks on end.

I think about people who have had it far worse than me; I rage because no one's ever had it this bad.

I cry until I hurt; I don't allow myself to cry.

I never watch any TV show that Lydia and I loved together; I binge on them for weeks.

It was knee-jerk, but it was always honest. If one were to collect the advice I've offered to the people who have reached out to me, it'd be a contradictory mess. You name it, I've tried it, am trying it, will try it. I don't know what to tell people about coping because the hurt is never gone. I never tell them there's hope or a timeline for overcoming such deep sorrow. I tell them matter-of-factly that it sucks and it will always suck and that the sooner you recognize that as the new reality, the sooner you'll adapt to it, whatever that looks like for you. Whatever defeated new landscape your life takes on. It's all very Russian.

But whenever people write to me concerned that someone they love is suicidal my advice is unflinching: it's not enough. What you're doing right now, it's not enough. Do more. Ask more questions. Drive them to more shrinks. Spend more nights watching them sob. I regret every time I rolled my eyes because Lydia was having another bad day. So much. I'm ashamed of myself for it. We all are. No matter how much we know it's not our fault, it doesn't matter. In our hearts, we feel guilty. I look back at Lydia's life and I'm sickened that we couldn't see it coming. A preternaturally intelligent girl who speaks backwards regularly, is sensitive and socially awkward, obsessed with dark literature and music and television, overdoses on sleeping pills and we thought she'd turn it around? What pills were *we* taking? "Deliberate indifference," I believe Anna and my dad would call it, borrowing a term from one of their many briefs taking down nursing homes or prison officials. As smart as we all are, as goddamn magnificent, why weren't we smart enough to see this sooner? Why couldn't we do anything to stop this?

It was impossible to put it all together in real time; it was impossible to prevent. Anna and I often console ourselves that way. We tell ourselves that if Lydia hadn't killed herself when she did, she would have done it some other time. Who knows how soon, but she would have done it just the same. And who knows what her life would have looked like then? Who knows if she would have been strung out on heroin or missing, leaving us playing the where's Lydia game for weeks, months, years. Christ, she could have had a child in the middle of all this. A motherless child.

My mom once shared her perspective with me. The way she saw it, she explained, modern science barely understands the human brain. All the studies, all the advancements, all the tests and pills and breakthroughs, it's all bullshit, she said. They still have such a rudimentary understanding of why the mind work the way it does. In a hundred years, doctors, scientists, psychiatrists, psychologists, they would look at Lydia and say, "Oh, this girl is clearly suffering from X, Y, and Z." And they would prescribe her the proper regimen, whatever it took to fix X, Y, and Z. Then off Lydia would go to fulfill her potential, to find a sense of worth, of happiness. But of course science isn't there yet. So all we're left with is the clumsy knowledge that Lydia suffered from . . . something. Something we were powerless to stop. It was mental illness—a real disease, as legitimate as any of the others. That's what got Lydia in the end. Not our ineptitude or lack of perception, the disease.

It helps to think this way, to view it as an inevitability that was neither Lydia's fault nor our own. It's the only way to free yourself from a prison of anguish. The only way to realize that despite all the suffering, even though she's not here anymore, you are.

L'ISLE-SUR-LA-SORGUE

I got back together with Katie. I had this sneaking suspicion she was the one, that I had tossed aside something amazing to focus on something awful. She met me for coffee downtown. I apologized. She was hurt, but she understood. I asked her to give our relationship another try. It took some convincing, but she finally agreed. I was so grateful. I missed her.

I can't imagine dealing with the emotional yo-yo that I had become. I needed someone to hold my hand and re-introduce me to the notion of joy. Katie did just that. At the same time, she was also demanding in the exact way that I needed. Comics are vain by nature. Add to that mix the depression that I wore like a burial shroud, and there wasn't much thinking that I was doing outside of myself. But Katie wouldn't tolerate that. She insisted that I show up, that I act like the partner that she needed. She reminded me that a relationship is not a one-way street, one I get to walk down obliviously while she tries to cheer me up. Time may have stopped for me the day that Lydia died, but Katie was there to remind me that the world kept turning. And if

I wanted it to turn with her by my side, I needed to be present. I could be broken, devastated, haunted, and she would be there to help me through it. But the one thing I couldn't be was absent.

She was like my shrink, the one that broke through: sympathetic but never pitying.

Her earnestness cut through me like a knife. I had become so nihilistic. I had doubled down on being the caustic smart-ass since Lydia's death. Katie wouldn't allow me to be that person. She wasn't interested in him. She was attracted to my better qualities.

She was unlike anyone I had ever gone for. So genuine and uncynical. So unassuming. She made me feel hopeful. When I looked at her I saw our children's crayon drawings beneath the magnets on our refrigerator. I was so grateful for the optimism she inspired in me.

Plus, she looks a lot like Nancy Kerrigan. Same big teeth. Same great legs. I really didn't have a choice.

Things kept looking up. I got booked to do Conan, a dream come true for the high school nerd who obsessed over *The Simpsons*; many of my favorite episodes were written by Conan specifically.

My whole family came with me. What remained of it. We made a real occasion out of it. My dad booked us at the Sunset Plaza, a fancy hotel for the stars. We saw Vince Vaughn and Tilda Swinton at the restaurant in the lobby. We were more impressed with the hotel literature, which informed us that when John Wayne lived there for a period, the hotel let him keep a dairy cow on the premises so he could have fresh cream for his morning coffee. The fucking Duke. That's the kind of celebrity I aspired to, I thought: folksy and insane.

When I got to Conan's studio on the Warner Bros. lot in LA they walked me through the motions. Here was the curtain behind which I would wait until Conan introduced me. There was the X on the floor where I was to stand, my mark. They instructed me on where to look during the taping, to not stare directly into the camera like a fucking creep; mostly they just urged me to have fun. To treat the room as I would any other comedy club and enjoy myself. The whole experience was so relaxed. I couldn't help but feel at ease. Until the show itself started, and it wasn't a dry run anymore. Then it was the real thing, replete with a live studio audience and LaBamba leading the band and Andy Richter walking around backstage, then suddenly Conan himself, tall and lanky and in total command. This was real. This was happening. No turning back now. Game face.

I sat there in my greenroom with a few comedy buddies sweating bullets. I took off my show-shirt so I wouldn't get pit stains and waited there in an undershirt, watching the show unfold on the closed-circuit monitor: Dax Shepard; some telenovela bombshell making the crossover into American TV. Then it was my turn.

"Mr. Cayton-Holland, we're ready for you."

I put my show-shirt back on and they led me over to

the spot they had previously shown me, the X on the floor. There were two stagehands there now, one on each side of the curtain. They couldn't have been more over it. I nervously tried to make small talk but they weren't having it. They wouldn't even make eye contact, they just stood there completely silent, bored and surly.

Congrat-u-fucking-lations, kid. I swear to god, if this shoot goes overtime I'm calling my rep.

I'm usually pretty cold-blooded when it comes to performing, but something got to me in that moment. The enormity of the situation. All that I had been through. The nerves took hold. Suddenly I didn't want to do it. A cavalcade of worst-case scenarios ripped through my head. What if I was so nervous I stuttered? What if I forgot a joke? What if the jokes didn't work? What if I passed out? What would Conan think if I blew it on his show? What would everyone back in the Denver comedy scene think? What would my parents and sister think? As they sat there in the audience, cringing through five minutes of dog shit, their son and brother wilting beneath the big studio lights?

I started talking to Lydia. I needed her. I needed to talk comedy right then and there. How I wish I could have run my set with her in the weeks leading up to that moment, tweaking every little wording, every tag, figuring out the perfect opening few words. But I didn't have that luxury. So she for damned sure better guardian angel me. I don't like to go to that well often. To put pressure on my dead sister to see me through something difficult. Because what if she doesn't? Does that mean she's not there for me? But in that moment I didn't care. I was panicking. I started talking to her.

Lydia, I need you with me, right now! Watch over me during this set. Make this go smoothly. Help me get through this, Lee. Please. I can't do this without you. After all you've put me through, you fucking owe me this one. Call in a favor, ask whoever you report to to help me with this one. Do whatever you have to do.

I looked up. Both stagehands were staring straight at me. That got their attention. The one on the right farted. Go time.

"Ladies and gentlemen, Adam Cayton-Holland!"

It was a hell of a set. YouTube it. Sure, there's a certain feral-ness in my eyes until I get that first laugh, a desperate deer-in-headlights kind of look. But after that first laugh, you can see me lock in. I'm no longer scared; the confidence takes hold as I plow through my jokes, garnering multiple applause breaks.

Oh, this is it? Just tell jokes in front of a room ready to laugh? I can do that! This is my wheelhouse.

"Great job," Conan said as he shook my hand. "Really funny stuff!"

It was the first we had spoken. I geeked out. I was on such a high. My late-night stand-up comedy debut! I did it. I fucking did it. It felt like a culmination; like everything I'd ever done in comedy led to that set and this was the moment I became a professional stand-up comic. Sure you could say I was one before that; I earned my living doing it, declared it on my taxes, all that. But *Conan* felt significant. I could die. I could never tell another joke again, that set would never go away.

They weren't sure if they needed another minute or two to fill out the episode so Conan invited me over to the couch. Back in the day, when a set on Johnny Carson meant a legit shot at superstardom, the couch was the most coveted prize in all of stand-up comedy. While telling jokes in front of that iconic curtain meant every eye in Hollywood was on you, being invited over to the couch meant Johnny was a fan. So much so that he wanted to talk to you more; to see what made you tick and give you more of a chance to shine. It was the gold stamp of approval. There was no higher honor.

Of course, those days are long gone. Today, a late-night clip amounts to nothing more than a banner day or two on social media, another credit to tattoo on your poster hanging in the lobby of a comedy club. But it still felt fucking cool. I sat closest to Conan, next to the telenovela minx and Dax Shepard, and Conan and I chatted about *The Simpsons*. I told him that my two favorite episodes were written by him.

" 'Monorail'?" he asked.

"That's one of them," I said. "But also 'Homer Goes to College.' "

"That's a deep cut," he said. "No one ever says that one."

I told him my favorite line. Homer is working on his college admissions package. He's glued a picture of himself to his essay: he's in a birthday hat, shoving an entire cake into his mouth. He writes the last line, reading it aloud:

"It was the most I ever threw up, and it changed my life forever."

Conan laughed at the memory. "Thanks, man," he said. "That's really cool of you to say."

They didn't use any of the footage. Just a shot of me with the other guests and Conan waving to the camera as the credits scroll. But it didn't matter. High school Adam would have shit a brick.

My dad and I took a trip to France a week later. My dad's been all over the globe, but Paris remains his favorite city. And he wanted to get back to it. He wanted to travel, to take in some of the world's beauty. My mom wasn't up for it yet; she was still hurting too bad. Anna couldn't get away because of work and her family. There wasn't a reason in the world I couldn't go. So father and son headed to France.

We spent five days in Paris splurging. We ate at fancy restaurants, checked out museums and shopped like the son and grandson of an art dealer that we are. Le Bon Marché, Forum des Halles. My dad bought expensive gifts for my mom; I bought jewelry for Katie. I called her one night, standing outside our hotel on the street.

"I love you," I said toward the end of the call.

It just came out of me. I had never told her that before,

but as soon as the words came out of my mouth I knew that they were true. She paused and a pregnant silence lingered in the air, across an ocean and many states.

"I love you, too," she said.

We took a train to Provence, made our way through Avignon and Aix-en-Provence, then to Arles where I made my father go because it was the last place poor little Vincent van Gogh lived. My dad followed me around the city as I told him all about Van Gogh's tragic ending: his cohabitation with gruff Gauguin, who was not only a dick but a successful one, selling paintings and swaggering, while the true genius of the duo poured brilliance into the canvas unnoticed and borrowed money from his brother Theo, his mind slipping further and further away. Such a sad, desperate ending for the greatest of the impressionists in that tiny yellow house. My dad knew all the details of the story as well but seemed slightly concerned at my fascination with it, wondering, no doubt, what exactly he had done to encourage such morbid children. It wasn't his fault. It's just in our DNA.

On the second-to-last day of the trip, before we checked into a hotel in Marseilles for one night and caught an early morning flight back to the States, we stopped into L'Isle-sur-la-Sorgue, a small village known for fine antiques. We parked the rental car in the central public lot and then milled about town for a few hours. When we came back to the car the rear windshield was smashed. And our luggage was gone. Both our suitcases, both our carry-ons. All the jewelry and clothing and fancy accoutrements from a lavish trip through France, stolen. My laptop and wallet and cell phone. Gone. Fortunately, we both had our passports on us, and my dad had his wallet. It was shocking. We went to the local police station and filed a report, my father speaking in broken French, the cop in broken English. We asked if there was any chance of recovering our items and were told quite bluntly that there was not. That stuff was probably on a boat by now, heading off to who knows where. The thieves had targeted our car because we had rental license plates. The police acted like it was our fault. Shouldn't drive a car with rental plates. Certainly not one loaded with all your luggage. We drove to Marseilles in silence, the wind howling through the nonexistent back windshield.

We stopped at a gas station for toothbrushes.

I was so mad. Here we were on this father-son trip to France, an attempt to celebrate life a little bit and put the death of our sister and daughter out of our minds, and what did we get in return? Fucking robbed. Had we not suffered enough? This just seemed cruel, a little extra slice of fuck-you. My dad didn't have any answers. He seemed equally distraught. But he offered enough positivity to pull me through it. We were fine. We had not been hurt. Insurance would cover everything. It was just a pain in the ass, nothing more. Those thieves probably needed the money they would get for selling our stuff more than we did.

He was right. But it was hard to stomach. We were both

walking an emotional tightrope. We felt violated. When the situation switched and my father became despondent, I propped him up. Parroted the same things he had said to comfort me. We yo-yoed like that all afternoon until we came away with the only conclusion one could come away with: this is life. The good goes hand in hand with the bad. One minute you're shaking hands with a childhood idol, the next moment you're getting kicked in the dick in France.

That night we walked down to the port, in the rain. Our hotel was close. They loaned us two umbrellas. The city was dead. But we kept our eyes peeled for imaginary pick-pockets and thieves. We were once-bitten, and paranoid. None surfaced. The streets were empty, and safe. There was hardly anyone at the port either, just a few tourists like ourselves. Yet all the restaurants were open, one after another, all eager for our business. We chose the one that felt the least touristy and sat in an outdoor tent with clear plastic windows that allowed us to gaze out at all the boats bobbing in the port.

Marseille is known for bouillabaisse, a traditional fish stew. We ordered a pot of it. It took forever so we sat there eating baskets of bread, listening to the rain pelt the tent as the storm picked up. Every few minutes a violent gust of wind would blow open the entrance flap, sending nap-kins and paper place mats flying. The waiters scurried to secure the entryway but it was futile. The flap would open, debris would fly everywhere, and the few customers inside would get soaked with a blast of rain. There was nothing any of us could do about it. So we ordered a bottle of wine to keep us warm. Fuck the early morning flight. We could have a little bit of a hangover. Not like we had any bags to check. When it was done we ordered another bottle. And we laughed every time the flap to the tent burst open, right in the face of the storm. Finally, the bouillabaisse came. And we devoured it. We didn't leave a drop. We took a cab back to the hotel instead of walking. We collapsed into our side-by-side twin beds and slept like the dead, father and son, safe and sound. The next morning, at the airport, everyone marveled at how lightly we traveled.

THE BENCH BY THE LAKE

The sadness, it never leaves you. The best you can hope for is to control it. Which I've mostly done. I've tried to channel my grief to appropriate times, and places. At the therapist's office, hikes in the mountains. Mostly I take it to the bench we got Lydia in City Park. We never buried her. We cremated her and she still sits in an urn on a closet shelf in my parents' house. But I needed a place to mourn, so I suggested we get her a bench. It's right by Bird Island, near a colony of black-crowned night herons that we used to laugh at, the way the white plumes on the backs of their heads stick up and make them look like little Einsteins. I thought getting the bench would be harder than it was, that the demand would be higher, but it was surprisingly easy. A few thousand bucks to Denver Parks and Recreation and we got to choose the location. A simple plaque reads, "IN LOVING MEMORY OF LYDIA ANN CAYTON-HOLLAND."

When I'm feeling sad and missing Lydia I go there to tell her about what I've been up to, what the family has been up to. I let my grief out. I try to force myself to feel everything. But sometimes it doesn't work. Sometimes I don't feel anything. And I've learned that's okay. It's a gradual acceptance. Her death is a part of my life, it can render me incapacitated or roll right off my back. My reaction can differ by the minute. And so on those days when I feel nothing I pick up the trash around her bench, I polish her plaque and make sure it's as pristine as possible and then I head on my way. I go back out into the city I love to work on a script at a coffee shop, or visit my older sister and my nephews and niece, or help my mom run some errands, or hang out with my dad at his office or listen to records with Katie in our living room. I take it all as it comes. I do my best to live my life without her.

I embrace those numb moments because this unfeeling never lasts too long. I can go for days, weeks even, without really thinking about Lydia being gone, but then suddenly it's right there again. And it's when it sneaks up on me that it hurts so much worse. An e-mail from an old friend of mine, or hers, who just somehow got the news through the grapevine. A photo posted on social media. A cashier at the pet store removing your punch card from the box behind the register—twelve bags of dog food, get one free.

"Cayton-Holland, got it! Lydia or Adam?"

Adam. There is no Lydia. Not anymore.

Those moments send me hurtling back.

Like the other day. Katie and I met my parents for lunch at a Mexican restaurant. We pulled into the parking lot a few minutes before my parents arrived and as we were exiting the car I blurted out, "I wonder if Lydia's coming."

And I meant it. The whole situation seemed so familiar, a Sunday lunch with my parents, some enchiladas and crispy chile rellenos, a bowl of green chile on the side. Of course Lydia would be there. She'd order three bean burritos, not smothered, and she'd take one of them home with her in a white Styrofoam to-go box. She'd drink two Cokes over the course of the meal and devour the chips and salsa. I'd experienced that scene a hundred times in my life. It was so normal and safe and rote, so real life, I could feel her there with us.

"You're kidding, right?" Katie asked, slightly concerned.

My frontal lobe took over. Oh yeah. Duh. Dead. No Lydia. Ever again. Not this meal, or the next one or the one twenty years from now. Not the next movie, not the next birthday, not the next coffee shop or comedy show or nephew's soccer game. Not at her wedding, or mine. Or the birth of her child. Or mine. She's just fucking gone. Forever.

Those moments feel like the first time every time. And unlike the memory of finding her body, I can't store them away tidily in some mental filing cabinet. They're too general, too broad. It's a sense of my little sister that I'm missing in those moments, a feeling, one that exists inside of me like DNA.

I had to sit down on the curb outside that Mexican restaurant and catch my breath. And I had to do it quickly, before my parents pulled into the lot. Lest they see me like that; lest I trigger them. The perpetual thin ice of a proud, devastated family, unable to show just how broken they are at times for fear of breaking the others.

And I'm so mad at Lydia in those moments, every time. And I'm so sad for her too. And for myself. And for my poor family. But there's not a lot you can do. There's nothing you can do, in fact.

So Katie and I went into the restaurant and we waited for my parents and when they arrived we caught up and none of us said a thing about Lydia's absence, which we all felt acutely, like we do every time. The moments we're not sad about her are but brief interruptions from a grief we've left on pause.

We just do the best we can.

MY SISTER, THE HAWK

I was at the bar after a show when my buddy's wife, Maggie, beelined over to me. She had a fire in her eyes. She had to talk to me, she said.

Okay.

Lydia was communicating to her, she said. Through her. Desperately begging her to talk to me, to communicate with me, to relay a message. Maggie was wild-eyed, her words were not coming out clearly. She started and stopped, stammered awkwardly as she tried to get out what she needed to say. She just had to tell me on behalf of Lydia that everything is okay. That she's with me.

I must have looked at her like I thought she was a fucking lunatic because she grabbed my hand and put it to her neck.

"Here," she said. "Feel my pulse."

It was throbbing, practically beating out of her neck. If it were me, I would have gone to the hospital immediately.

"Jesus, Maggie!" I blurted out. "Are you okay?"

She couldn't even answer. Her husband, Drew, intervened. We used to write at the newspaper together. He's a cynical journalist type, a policer of all things bullshit; he knew exactly how I would react to his wife approaching me and discussing communicating with my little sister from beyond the grave. He quickly did his best to calm Maggie down, and then he tried to assuage my doubts.

"I called bullshit on it too, initially," he said of his wife's ability to tap into something higher. "But there's been so many times where I've been proven wrong by her, eventually I just kind of accepted it."

We talked it out for a few minutes and after a while Maggie calmed down. Her pulse returned to normal. She told me that she is just starting to understand this weird gift she has. She called it "energy work" and explained that she often feels the pulse of what people are feeling, or what people are working through. She said it has always been the case for her but only recently was she attempting to understand it, to learn how to talk about it, maybe even harness or tame it. But it's still all very overwhelming for her, she said.

I had no idea what to say. I've known Drew and Maggie for years. They're no flakes. But this was so out of left field, so hippy-dippy. And truthfully, I didn't want to talk about it. I felt bombarded. I just wanted to tell some dick jokes in my friend's new bar and then get hammered. The last thing I wanted was to discuss Lydia. Especially in some new-agey, spiritual manner that I had never asked for or invited. With someone whom I was a friendly acquaintance with, but hardly someone I would turn to about such matters.

I told Maggie thank you for talking to me and that we should discuss this further sometime. I didn't mean it. I just wanted out. The next morning, she texted me a quasi apology and I wrote her back saying she had nothing to apologize for. And that was that. I didn't reach out to her and she didn't reach out to me. But I kept thinking about it.

Even though I'm a cynical comic, I've never shut the door to things like meditation, yoga, tapping into a higher power. And unlike most of my friends I'm always careful to label myself an agnostic, not an atheist. Because an atheist assumes they know. And that's always been my problem with religion. How do you know? How does anyone know? I like not knowing. It seems more honest. My belief system was grounded in that simple truth my father taught me as a child, when Wade died and he pulled a picture book of the universe from the shelf. No one knows. But isn't it amazing that we get to experience it all? And even if experiencing it all had lost its appeal for me, I still clung to the belief that no one knew. Since Lydia's death I had embraced the mystery. Which made anything seem possible.

Like the idea of Lydia becoming a red-tailed hawk.

Our first encounter was a day or two after her funeral. My uncle Lauren was still staying at our house with his family, there for his sister, my mom, as best he could be. He let the dog out into the backyard and noticed a red-tailed hawk perched in our crab apple tree. It just sat there, totally nonplussed by his presence. There was something strange in its stillness. He showed my mom, who in turn showed me, and we all agreed there was something different about the bird. It was atypically calm. We speculated that maybe it was injured, or just a confused juvenile, not yet comfortable in its skin. But we couldn't stop staring at it. It was so peaceful, so serene. We watched as a squirrel climbed the tree and joined it on the branch. The hawk could care less. The two of them just sat there, predator and prey, side by side. They remained there together until we went inside.

"Something's off about that hawk," my uncle concluded. We didn't give it any further thought.

A few weeks later my mom came home from running errands and parked her car on the side street alongside the house. Something fluttered through her field of vision. She whirled around to follow it and was surprised to see that a red-tailed hawk had landed on the roof of her car. It stared at her. She stared back. Then it began rubbing its head on the car, over and over again. Bending low, twisting its neck so that the top of its head brushed the metal of the car, then returning to its normal, upright position. It would hold its position like that for seconds, bowing low, submissive. She had never seen a bird behave that way. It seemed to be offering itself up for consideration, lying prostrate before her, as though my mother were queen of the red-tails. My mom was overcome. She remembered the strange hawk encounter from before.

"Lydia?" she asked.

The bird just stared at her. Then it flew away.

Of course, my mother only related this to me when I

told her of my separate encounter. We were casting for the pilot of *Those Who Can't* in an office space on the west side of town, right on the Platte River. The room we were in had one wall that essentially was a large, glass window through which we overlooked the entire complex. Suddenly a hawk shot past, then swopped low over the parking lot and landed on a fence some two hundred yards away. It was a slow point in the day anyway so I ran outside to get a better look. As I got close to the hawk, still perched on a fence, it stared at me, not with anger or fear, but a look I can only describe as knowing. Like we were familiar. I crept closer, a foot or two at a time. Soon I was so close that with a sudden move I felt as if I could touch it. The raptor never faltered, never flinched. Then it turned away from me so it was facing out, over a field, perhaps scanning for prey. I figured it would fly off but then it did something I've never seen a bird do to this day. It stretched both its wings wide and held them there, like the iconic Aztec eagle. It didn't flap them, it didn't stretch them out and then pull them back into its slender, powerful body. It kept them completely outstretched, in profile, as if to say *behold*. I stared in awe.

"Lydia?" I asked.

The hawk turned its head and looked back at me, held its steely gaze. Then it flew away.

I went back into the office, moved, but didn't share what had happened. I just reported how close I had gotten to the hawk. But when I shared the story with my mother, she looked at me with wide eyes and we both just knew. That was her. That was Lydia. Just like it had been that day with my uncle. There was no doubt in our minds. We held no deep understanding of reincarnation. We couldn't even say whether or not we believed we saw the same hawk. We just felt Lydia's presence in those encounters and for us that was enough to believe. She was trying to reach us. She was trying to show us how beautiful and strong she still was. We saw red-tailed hawks all the time after that. In fairness they're common, but the frequency was uncanny.

On her first birthday after she died, on the day she would have turned twenty-nine, I went to visit her bench. When I got there someone was already sitting on it, enjoying their day in the park. I liked that. Lydia had become a part of the park we were raised in, like a swing set on a playground, or an animal in the zoo. Or a gnome hidden in the museum walls. There was so much mystery and wonder right there in our backyard, if only people knew to look for it.

I left the woman alone on Lydia's bench and went and lay down beneath a tree to try to wait her out. I'd visit Lydia's bench after. As I lay there staring up into the branches a bird flew into the tree. I jumped up and tried to identify it, circling the trunk to get a better angle. Sure enough, red-tailed hawk. I couldn't believe it. Had that person not been sitting on Lydia's bench I would have never lain beneath that tree. And my hawk little sister would never have paid me a visit. It wasn't too hard to convince myself that she had led me there all along.

A few days after my wedding to Katie, where Anna was a bridesmaid and Lydia was not, Maggie wrote me a lengthy e-mail. I later learned that she was waiting until after my wedding to contact me again. She didn't want to bother me with missives from my dead little sister as I was preparing for what should be one of the happiest days of my life.

> Your sister had been in my heart a number of times before we talked that night, after your show. It was a haunting but comfortable feeling, and for some reason I always knew when it was her. There was this one time that I was working with a healer, and she said, "There is a woman who died very young here with you." And right away, I knew it was Lydia. I asked the woman who was helping me if she was my friend's sister and she said yes, it certainly was.

I didn't know what to think. I kept reading.

> When I saw you after your show, I had no idea what was coming was coming. But once it started, I had no control. I spent some time after that night thinking about and coming to a better understanding of what happened, and how her energy took over mine. So here goes. You may remember my pulse. That felt insane inside my body, to have it all come on so quickly, like I had done wind sprints, and then to have it come back to

normal moments later, once I released Lydia's words to you. That was her excitement coming out. I am certain that she was so excited to have a way to communicate with you in a way she knew for sure that you would hear. Over the next few days, I think what I learned is that you ask her hundreds of questions, big ones about life choices, and little ones too, like which socks to wear, and once she knew I had you open to listening, she tried to answer every question you had ever asked all at once, and that was why my pulse went crazy, because I had never experienced that type of input.

I embraced the possibility. I couldn't recall if I was asking Lydia questions or not. But I was talking to her all the time, in my own inner monologue, whether it was seated on her bench in the park or when I was on a jog. In those absentminded moments when you snap to after who knows how long of your brain wandering, I'd realize I had been carrying on a conversation with Lydia in my head. Maggie described herself in the e-mail as "an empath." That resonated deeply. Because that was what Lydia was. *An empath.* I never had a word for it, but there it was. Someone who feels and commiserates to a level that may not even be healthy. Maggie said that as an empath, grief and suffering were some of the easiest things to pick up on. I thought of Lydia and her love of animals, her desire to not even see plants suffer. Was that why Lydia was reaching out to Maggie? Because they were both so empathetic?

Maggie said she could tell I was covered in grief. And Lydia could too. She could tell our whole family was still reeling. And that was driving my little sister crazy. That made her so sad. She didn't want that for me. She didn't want that for any of us. So she was reaching out to Maggie constantly to help me. Maggie didn't know why Lydia was choosing her. She had met Lydia a handful of times but had no real relationship with her. She knew her merely as the nice little sister of Adam, nothing more. But Maggie figured Lydia simply was going for the person closest to me who was receptive to hearing such messages. I wondered if those times she had visited my mother and me in hawk form were before she found Maggie.

Everything Maggie was writing hit home so hard. And that scared me. Was this who I was now? Someone who believed in energy work and chakras? Someone who thought the dead spoke to us? Should I drive up to Boulder and hang out at Naropa? Buy lots of turquoise and start offering strangers shoulder massages on the Pearl Street Mall? I didn't care. Everything Maggie was saying, I wanted to hear so badly. I kept reading.

The next thing I need to convey to you is that she is trying very hard to answer you. She wants you to know that she hears you when you are talking to her. Her means of communication are harder to interpret but if you open your heart a little wider you might find comfort in the little answers. Maybe a picture is tilted, something seems to not be in its usual place, an electronic behaves strangely, the lights flicker oddly when you turn them on or off. Be open to accepting that her energy is there with you.

I called Maggie a few days afterward. We talked for almost two hours. I learned things about Maggie I had never known. Like how her father died when she was five from cancer. He was diagnosed when her mother was pregnant with her. He was given six months to live, but he made it his goal to make it to the birth of his daughter. And he lived five years past that goal. Maggie always felt connected with her dad, but soon after he died she said she got a message from him. She relayed it to her mother.

Second drawer of the china hutch.

She didn't understand what it meant but she told her mom that her dad had told her to pass it along. Her mother looked in that drawer. It was their life insurance policy. She had been ransacking the house looking for it. The policy was expiring soon.

Ever since that day, Maggie felt she was more attuned, more tapped in to something bigger than herself. There were a dozen other such experiences over the course of her life confirming her suspicion. In her family, it was just an accepted truism: Maggie understands things on a higher level. She explained that her numerous experiences were rarely as clear a message as the second drawer of a china hutch, but they were these powerful feelings that would come over her nonetheless. And Lydia was something she was feeling as powerfully as anything she had in a long while.

And it persisted. Maggie told me that after that night of my show, Lydia kept harassing her. More than ever before. She needed to talk to me more, but Maggie kept putting it off. She knew how weird it would all sound. And she didn't want to bother me before my wedding. She felt like she had already bothered me too much that night. But the day after my wedding, she started feeling this nonstop pressure from Lydia to reach out again. She and Drew went home to Wisconsin for Thanksgiving—while I was on my honeymoon—and for the entire thousand-mile drive back to Colorado Lydia hounded her to reach out to me. Maggie described it as this persistent, nagging voice:

You said you were going to talk to him after the wedding. It's after the wedding. Why haven't you talked to him? Are you going to talk to him at all? When are you going to talk to him?

She said it kept her from sleeping it was so relentless. That sounded like Lydia all right.

"Okay, Maggie," I said bluntly. "You've got my ear. I'm listening. What does Lydia have to say?"

"She loves you so much," Maggie said, unfazed at my rude tone, relieved to finally be unburdening herself of my little sister's message. "And she walks every step of your path with you. She is so proud of you and so peaceful about the direction you are heading."

Maggie told me about a vision she had the day of Lydia's

funeral. Maggie was there that day, with Drew. Her description was one of energies and darkness and light. A large black umbrella engulfed the service, she said; it was like this cosmic shroud that hung over Anna's entire house. It was my mother's suffering, the heaviest, blackest pain anyone could ever imagine. From the south, descending upon the funeral, Maggie noticed a matching dark umbrella. This was Lydia's energy, Maggie explained. And Lydia was feeling so sad for what she had done, what she had to do. The two black clouds met and became one directly over the house. In Maggie's vision the backyard became shrouded in black, a sort of cosmic darkness that formed a dome underneath which we all sat. But over the course of the service, that dome began to fill with the brightest white light that only pure love produces. Maggie said she could see myself and Anna and my father begin to release our own darkness and shine. And then she watched as my mother finally joined the funeral in progress, shining with her own white radiance. And Maggie said she watched as we all began to literally glow with the love and peace of knowing that although we all have this darkness now, to carry with us forever, Lydia's was no longer there. We took it on for her. She relinquished it to us. Maggie said she sat in that backyard and watched us shine in the subconscious knowledge that Lydia's pain was no longer heavy; that there was no more suffering for the girl we loved with every ounce of our being.

"She has peace," Maggie said. "So give yourself permission to find your own. And keep your eyes and your heart wide open because she is trying so hard to make sure you see her. If you feel a tingle and you think something might be her . . . it is."

"So what now?" I asked, tears streaming down my face. "What do I do now?"

Maggie didn't hesitate.

"That's completely up to you."

THE TATTOOED LADY

My dad and I were playing catch in the front yard of my childhood house, two postcard Americans, father and son. It was a bright Sunday. Neighbors walked by and made quaint remarks.

Is spring here already?!

You guys going out for the Rockies this year?!

People always like seeing us out there. There's something timeless about it. As they walked by I wondered how many of them knew our story. I wondered if any of them saw Lydia and Anna and me out there when we were kids, setting up lemonade stands and making snowmen. Did they see us trailing after our mom like baby ducks all those years, helping her unload groceries from the car? Did they know what happened to the little girl? Did any of them want to say anything? Offer their condolences? Were the ones who just kept their heads down searching for the words?

"You know what I've realized lately?" my dad asked me, both of our fastballs picking up velocity as our arms loosened up.

"What's that?" I asked.

"That I'm just so over the bullshit of all of it," he said.

I asked him what he meant.

"The bullshit. The dark stuff, the bad stuff. Remembering the death itself and the trips to the hospital and the feelings of pain and guilt and all of that. I'm so sick of thinking about it. I could not be more done with all of that."

I could relate. I had been writing this book. Thinking about her too much. Thinking about too much of the bad stuff.

"I just *miss* her," he said.

It's been six years since Lydia's death, and we're all trying so hard to grieve and to mourn and process everything we've been through. Some days are successes, others painful failures. It's hard to even keep track.

I just miss her.

I do too. I miss everything about her.

"Three pushes," my dad would often say when he was teasing Lydia. "Best at being born."

That's all it took, by my dad's account anyway. Three pushes from my mom and out she came, wide-eyed, excitable, ready for the world. Like she couldn't wait to join her family and get started. I think she lived her life that way. With that urgency.

The way she spoke. So fast. So intense. If you didn't get the first word in with Lydia, forget about it. That was your only shot. If you did, Lydia was gracious. Happy to listen, happy to hear about everything you wanted to bring to the table and offer informed opinions and advice. But if Lydia took the reins of a conversation you were off full clip down whatever rabbit hole she was currently occupying. But it was endearing. She was such a gifted thinker, so nimble and eloquent, before you knew it you couldn't help but agree that yes, *Firefly* is the most important television show of the early 2000s and anyone who doesn't see that is not only fooling themselves but completely wasting your time.

She was an obsessive in the best sense of the word. I never saw my grandfather the art dealer in action. But his handiwork was the backdrop of my childhood. And it's clear that the man was gifted; that he had far-ranging, eclectic tastes and truly appreciated the artists with whom he formed relationships. I imagine that he must have gotten lost in the art, consumed by it. It's not hard to see that in Lydia. In the way she went about truly appreciating things. That's why in spite of her crippling inability to harness her natural gifts, her circle was always dominated by musicians and artists. She got it. She understood. Often better than the artists themselves.

She fixated. It was unwavering.

I loved watching her fixate.

There were no casual interests for her. If something attracted her attention, she would follow it until there was literally nowhere else to turn. And if she could tell you about it then she was truly at her happiest. She loved sharing her obsessions, she loved turning you on to them: *The Tick*, the Misfits, the Coen Brothers. But even if her tastes weren't cool, she pursued them wholesale. It did not matter the popular perception. If she liked it, that was all that mattered. She was unapologetic. I've never met someone so detached from cultural peer pressure. Hipsters withered at her feet. She was cynical, but never ironic. Her friend told me once when they were riding an escalator down to a parking garage after a movie, Lydia started doing high-kicks and singing "Magical Mister Mistoffelees" from *Cats*. She was in her twenties. Some guy watching her was so charmed by the whole thing he asked her out. Lydia and her friend gushed about it the whole way home. She was unapologetically herself.

I loved watching Lydia interact with animals.

She was a Doolittle. She whispered to them. She cooed. And they all responded. Lucy her hedgehog. Pipkin her rabbit. Penelope her greylag goose that she hatched in freshman biology as an experiment on imprinting. All the other geese were taken to some farm after the experiment. Imprinting be damned. Not Penelope. She stayed with us. Lived in our backyard, a real neighborhood attraction.

Lydia's cat was her greatest joy: Sugar, an athletic, stray crow-assassin that we took in one Halloween night. Sugar was at her beck and call. Lydia would sing her name out and Sugar would come running. Even if she was outside, she'd shoot in through the cat door, track Lydia down, and nimbly jump into her arms. Lydia would boost Sugar up on her shoulders, front paws on one side, back paws on the other, her torso up against the back of Lydia's head so she wore her like a high collar. They would walk around like that: Lydia with her Sugar-scarf. Sugar liked all of us; Sugar loved Lydia. When Sugar died Lydia got a tattoo on her right collarbone of Sugar's paw print. A collarbone that has since been incinerated and sits with the rest of her, in a jar, in her closet.

My little sister.

I loved watching Lydia eat.

It was fascinating. She would latch on to one food and eat it obsessively for weeks on end. Sautéed spinach with lemon and garlic for three weeks straight. MorningStar Farms Chik'n Nuggets for the next two. She loved Carmine's on Penn, a family-style, high-end Italian place in Denver. Lydia would order take-out minestrone and baked ziti and a basket or two of their complimentary rolls, haul the ten-pound to-go order back to her house, and subsist on it for weeks: a stick-thin, hundred-pound glutton feasting in front of *Buffy* reruns like a mob boss. There was always a grocery store sheet cake in her fridge. Always. And of course all this was supplemented with a steady regimen of Goldfish crackers and mint Milanos, which she consumed with appalling frequency. Pepperidge Farm ought to build a statue of Lydia, somewhere out in the fields of Genevas and Pirouettes. So should Coca-Cola. Next to the statue of Jordan dunking. She drank three Cokes a day. Easily. Not Diet Coke, straight up Coca-Cola Classic, ole faithful, the fucking good stuff. And yet her teeth didn't rot out of her head. And she didn't have diabetes. It powered her, coursed through her body like oil in a truck. She could have been the poster child for Coke. You would have loved watching the satisfaction with which she would drink it. You would have loved to hear how powerfully she could belch afterward. My god. It was incredible.

I loved having Lydia love me.

There was no one more loyal. Her love was total and irrefutable. She held nothing back. Your happiness was hers. So was your suffering. Which she could not stand; which she would do anything to remedy. When we were kids we would play *Oregon Trail* on our Apple IIGS. But we could never pack our family into a covered wagon and head out west to meet our fate. We could never punch in John and Linda and Anna and Adam and Lydia as players at the beginning of the game and then head off down the trail. Because sickness and suffering awaited us, and Lydia couldn't stand that, even fictionally. It was far easier on her to invent characters. She could handle Marcus dying of dysentery outside of Fort Kearney. Adam not so much. That's how much she loved us.

That's how I know she had to do what she did.

She loved us so goddamn much and she knew how much we loved her and how devastating it would be to us if she took herself out of the equation, yet she did it anyway. The thought of us hurting and suffering hurt her so badly and yet she still killed herself. She caused us hurt and suffering. That's how I know there was no other choice for her. She knew she would destroy us but she had to do it anyway. Her pain was that great. And if that's the choice she had to make to end the misery, then I have to choose to love her for that choice. She loved me unconditionally and I must do the same. We all must do the same.

Lydia was so much more than the broken, scared girl she was so often toward the end. She wasn't always confused and sad and haunted. For most of her life, she glowed. She was this awesome original; this strange, funny, powerful force. There was no changing Lydia; it became a point of pride. There was no telling her how it was going to be for her, what she should or could be doing. And there was power in that. We all begrudgingly respected Lydia as immutable, whether we agreed with her or not. Right or wrong, we were impressed with her will, with the sheer force of her being. And we loved her for it. We love her for it still.

GOODNIGHT, MOON

My OCD has gotten better. It's not nearly as crippling as it once was. Still, there are some rituals that remain, rituals that must be adhered to. Airplanes, for example. I have a regimen. I fly so much now, how could I not? I always have to buy a bottle of water for the flight. I always have to have gum. Both items must be stored away in my backpack for me to be able to get onboard. And when I do board the plane, as I'm transferring from the jet bridge onto the actual jet itself, I must touch the outside of the plane, I must feel the cool fuselage on my fingertips.

I always take a window seat toward the back, behind the wing. Somewhere I heard that that portion of the plane fares better in a crash. I have no idea if this is true or not, but I adhere to it anyway as a rule. Were someone to correct me on this notion, it wouldn't matter. My routine would remain unchanged. It's been established now. I leave my backpack in my window seat before I ever sit down, and I go to the bathroom before the plane takes off. I do this whether I need to or not. Who knows when I'll be able to get back up and visit the restroom again? What if the guy in the middle seat falls asleep, trapping me? So I pee. I wash my hands. Then I head back to my seat. I check the emergency instructions laminate like Anna taught me and after that, once I finally settle in and we're about to take off, I whisper the same, silent prayer that I've whispered for the past one hundred flights.

Dear Lord, please bless this vessel and all who dwell within it; please see it safely off the ground and safely back down to it.

I repeat this prayer before we land. To a god I cannot name and whom I often wonder if I even believe in. Doesn't matter. The results are undeniable. Haven't been in an airplane crash yet. Not one.

Knock on wood.

When I close down the house for the night, I have rituals as well. They're not nearly as neurotic as the ones I had when I was a kid, with the fours and the nines on the TV and the counting of the bars of the bed frame. It's a more casual routine, one probably familiar to many. The practical matters of turning in. I let the dogs outside to go to the bathroom. I go out with them, no matter how cold it is. I take a quiet moment for myself. I look up at the constellations: Orion, Cassiopeia. I remember how we don't know what any of it means. Or why. And I'm okay with that. I have to be. On cold nights I watch my breath and listen to my silent neighborhood. Except on Sundays, when the coal trains pass through town, a dozen or so blocks away, blowing their horns in the distance.

I let the dogs back in and they run upstairs and climb

into their doggy beds, next to my bed, where my wife lies, waiting for me. I remain downstairs, alone. My routine isn't finished yet. I check all the dials on the oven, one, two, three, four. All turned to the "off" position. No fires tonight. I turn off the light by the back door. Then the kitchen lights. Then the ones in the living room. Finally, I turn off the light in the front entrance, a chandelier, six bulbs. They normally shut right off, but sometimes, they flicker. Or hiss, as if swelling in intensity, in wattage. Sometimes they don't respond to the switch for several seconds, then they'll go off on their own. I've seen them turn off, turn back on, then turn off themselves, without me ever having touched the switch except for that first time. I watch in those moments and I try to feel her. I try as hard as I can. The lights do their strange little dance and I watch them and marvel, silent and uncomprehending.

Hi, Lee.

EPILOGUE

It's the summer a year before Lydia's death, a cool, bright day. For the most part, she's good. Happy. Funny. Beautiful. Haunted. Same old Lydia. She's back in the city she grew up in and seems to be enjoying it as an adult. She's vivid and alive.

Lydia's fished my mother's bike out of our parents' garage, tuned it up and taken to riding around the city, day and night. She keeps hounding me to bike with her but I'm traveling more for comedy, the leisure time eludes me. One Sunday I finally cave. Lydia rides over to my house and then walks her bike alongside me the few blocks to Denver Health. I rent a bike from the bike-share kiosk outside the hospital, the same hospital that I'll carry Lydia into a year from now. Just a few miles, I tell her. I've got stuff to do. We start off down the Cherry Creek bike path. It's gorgeous out, golden; Denver always shows off in the summer. Quickly we're at Confluence Park, where the city was settled. We cross the bridge over the confluence and bike northeast along the Platte River, toward Nebraska. Soon we've left the city behind us and are pushing into outer neighborhoods, then industrial ones, ones the gentrifiers haven't yet reached, then prairie. Lydia asks if I want to turn back; if I need to get to whatever it is I need to get to. I tell her we're good. Let's just keep going. It's too perfect out to stop.

We take a break across the Platte from Riverside Cemetery, home to the city's founding fathers with their elaborate tombs and mausoleums and monuments—decaying statues of uniformed men on horseback. We stop because we both notice something moving on the hillside, a half-dozen tiny, bobbing shapes. Focusing our eyes, we both realize they're wild turkeys, a whole messy gang of them, ambling east toward the cemetery. Neither Lydia nor I have ever seen turkeys in Denver. We observe them in a sort of reverent silence, watching them as they crest the hill and disappear from view.

"When I die I want to be buried in that cemetery," I tell Lydia apropos of nothing.

She nods solemnly. It's settled.

We don't turn back until we've reached Commerce City and the bike path fizzles out. We reverse course and retrace our ride, passing all the same sites, checking for the same turkeys by the cemetery, who have vanished. At the Confluence Park transfer from the Platte back to Cherry Creek, Lydia's bike gets away from her for a moment. Riding behind her I watch as she drops her feet from the pedals and skids to an abrupt stop against a fence, the handlebars driving her fingers into the banister. She cries out.

"You okay?" I ask when I catch up. Her knuckles are bloody. I help her manipulate each finger, making sure none of them are broken. They're not.

"I'm fine," she says, shaking her hands and hopping back on her bike. "That was fucking stupid."

She's tough, my little sister, I think as we head back toward our neighborhood.

We all are.

When I check my rental bike back in to the kiosk, Lydia gets off her bike and walks with me back to my house, the same path we will walk a year from now, after her overdose, after we throw away the pills. But nothing is farther from our minds, not her impending demise, not the dark thoughts we've both struggled to fight off our whole lives, the ones I silenced, the ones she's beginning to lose her battle with. None of that is there in that moment. We're just a big brother and a little sister walking through our neighborhood, side by side, on a beautiful summer evening. We've got so many days left together.

ACKNOWLEDGMENTS

I'd like to thank all the people who made this book possible, two in particular: my incredible agent Yishai Seidman for tracking me down in the land of podcasts and saying, "Hey, you should write a book," and my gifted editor Lauren Spiegel for knowing exactly when and how to push me and for making this book the best it could possibly be.

The greatest of love and thanks to my mom, dad, and sister Anna. Thank you for understanding that this memoir was part of my mourning process and for allowing me to do it. Your support and encouragement mean the world to me. I love you all with everything I've got. You are truly the Magnificent Cayton-Hollands, of which there will be five, never four, and I'm constantly blown away and inspired by all of you. I hope I have given readers of this book even a whisper of how incredible you each are. And Anna, thanks for having such great kiddos. They're just the best.

To my amazing wife, Katie: thank you, baby. So much. You've helped me through all of this in ways you're not even aware of, not just the writing of the book, but all of it. Thank you for pointing me toward the light every day. Thank you for making me optimistic. I love you.

And thanks for all the coffee.

To Lydia, I hope you like this book. I hope you feel it does you justice. Mere pages could never contain the charm and the wit and the humor that you brought to your life, but I tried. It was such an honor to get to be your brother, Lee. You were such a great sister. And daughter. And friend. Everyone who took the time to get to know you came away profoundly affected. You were a total fucking original. That's about the highest compliment I can give. I wish I could have had so many more years with you, but I'm grateful for every second that I had. So thank you. I love you. And I miss you so much. See you on the other side.

ABOUT THE AUTHOR

Adam Cayton-Holland is a writer, comic, and actor who lives in Denver, Colorado, with his wife, Katie, and his Chesapeake Bay retriever, Annabel Lee. Adam was named one of *Esquire*'s "Twenty-Five Comics to Watch," as well as one of "Ten Comics to Watch" by *Variety*. He is also the cocreator and star of *Those Who Can't*, in which Adam plays Spanish teacher and bon vivant Loren Payton. His albums *I Don't Know If I Happy*, *Backyards* and *Adam Cayton-Holland Performs His Signature Bits*, are all available on iTunes, and his writing has appeared in the *Village Voice*, *Spin*, *The A.V. Club*, and *The Atlantic*. He once threw out the opening pitch at a Colorado Rockies game, and people have described him as "genial" and "with pretty decent teeth." (www.adamcaytonholland.com)